COOK *and the* PACIFIC

With essays by JOHN MAYNARD,
SUSANNAH HELMAN AND MARTIN WOODS

NLA PUBLISHING

This book accompanied the exhibition *Cook and the Pacific* at the National Library of Australia from 22 September 2018 to 10 February 2019. The National Library thanks its generous supporters:

Australian Government
National Collecting Institutions
Touring & Outreach Program

ActewAGL for you

PRATT FOUNDATION

Kenyon Foundation

Title: Cook and the Pacific
Authors: Susannah Helman, John Maynard, Martin Woods
ISBN: 9780642279231
Published by NLA Publishing
Canberra   ACT   2600

Curatorial team: Dr Susannah Helman, Dr Martin Woods and Hollie Gill
Editor: Dr Robert Nichols
Designer: Amy Cullen
Production coordinator: Melissa Bush
Printed by CanPrint Communications Pty Limited

Find out more about NLA Publishing at publishing.nla.gov.au.

A catalogue record for this
book is available from the
National Library of Australia

FRONT COVER

John Cleveley (c. 1745–1786)
Discovery and Resolution at an island in the Pacific 1777 (detail) c. 1780s
Pictures Collection, National Library of Australia, Canberra,
PIC Screen 106 #T349

Banner Graphic: Commission, Michel Tuffery, Wellington, Aotearoa
New Zealand, 2018

FRONT COVER FLAPS

William Sharp (engraver, 1749–1824),
after John Webber (artist, 1752–1793)
A Night Dance by Men in Hapaee (detail) 1784
Pictures Collection, National Library of Australia, Canberra,
PIC Drawer 87 #U1245 NK10975/5

CONTENTS

Minister's Foreword v

Foreword vii

'I'm Captain Cooked': Aboriginal Perspectives on James Cook, 1770–2020
by John Maynard 1

Cook and the Pacific
by Susannah Helman and Martin Woods 5

Chapter 1: Who is James Cook and Where Did
He Come From? 18

Chapter 2: Navigating the Pacific 28

Chapter 3: Totaiete Mä 47

Chapter 4: South Pacific 62

Chapter 5: New Holland 86

Chapter 6: North Pacific 114

Chapter 7: Collecting Cook 132

Chapter 8: Cook After Cook 158

Endnotes 180

Further Reading 181

Index 182

Acknowledgements 184

MINISTER'S FOREWORD

Senator the Hon. Mitch Fifield,
Minister for the Arts

In 2018 we mark the 250th anniversary of the departure of HMB *Endeavour* from England on its journey of exploration of the Pacific. The voyage traversed the globe, reaching South America, the Society Islands, New Zealand, and the east coast of Australia before returning to England in 1771.

The expedition was led by one of the eighteenth century's greatest navigators, James Cook. He was accompanied on this voyage by gentleman scientist Joseph Banks, botanists Daniel Solander and Herman Spöring, astronomer Charles Green, and artists Alexander Buchan and Sydney Parkinson. This team of natural scientists and artists recorded observations, collected specimens and made sketches. They documented examples of flora and fauna never seen before in the old world. Their accounts of new lands and peoples were eagerly awaited at home.

Coinciding with the 50th anniversary of the National Library of Australia building, *Cook and the Pacific* will be shown exclusively at the Library in Canberra from 22 September 2018 to 10 February 2019.

Cook and the Pacific revisits Cook and his complex legacy. Drawing on some of the best Cook collections around the world, the exhibition will allow audiences to debate, question and explore the man and the myth. The exhibition will also provide an ideal forum to contribute to the national conversation about what Cook means to Australia, including how he was perceived at the time, how Indigenous people responded to Cook and how he is remembered today.

FOREWORD

Dr Marie-Louise Ayres, Director-General,
National Library of Australia

In 1923 the Australian Government purchased James Cook's *Endeavour Journal* at a sale in London. Sotheby, Wilkinson & Hodge were selling a collection of 'very important manuscript[s] by or relating to Captain James Cook, explorer', which had belonged to the late H.W.F. Bolckow, Esq., MP of Marton Hall, Yorkshire. Now known as the Library's MS 1, the volume is the most famous object its collection. It is the most complete copy of Cook's journal for his *Endeavour* voyage of 1768–71, in his own handwriting. In 2001 the journal became the first Australian item to be included on UNESCO's Memory of the World Register.

The purchase of the *Endeavour* journal is part of a larger story of how the Library built a magnificent and internationally renowned collection of original material relating to the three Pacific voyages of Captain Cook. The astonishing collections of E.A. Petherick, acquired in 1909, included a large collection of papers once belonging to Sir Joseph Banks. William Hodges' striking chalk portraits of Pacific people met on the second Pacific voyage (1772–75) were presented to the Library by the British Admiralty in 1939. Among the vast collections of Rex Nan Kivell, acquired in instalments between the 1950s and the 1970s, are pictures by voyage artist John Webber and George Carter's large oil painting *Death of Captain Cook* (1781). In 1985 the Library bought three lots at a London sale of the papers of John Montagu, 4th Earl of Sandwich. And the Library has continued to collect all things Cook.

Together these collections are an invaluable resource for exploring the history of Australia. They represent one of the world's best collections of manuscripts, works of art and objects relating to Cook's three Pacific voyages. The 250th anniversary of the *Endeavour* voyage provides a great opportunity to present this remarkable

collection to the Australian public. *Cook and the Pacific* is enriched with treasures from around the world. We are extremely grateful to our international lenders: The National Archives (UK), The British Library, London; Royal Society, London; National Maritime Museum, Greenwich, London; Natural History Museum, London; Captain Cook Memorial Museum, Whitby; Museum of New Zealand Te Papa Tongarewa, Wellington; Alexander Turnbull Library, Wellington; and the Bernice Pauahi Bishop Museum, Honolulu. Equally we are indebted to museums, libraries and private collectors across Australia who have been very generous in making available some of their most important Cook items for this exhibition.

I acknowledge the generous funding provided by the Australian Government through the Cook 250 and NCITO programs. Without this support, the exhibition would not have been possible. And I thank our sponsors, ActewAGL, the Kenyon Family Foundation, and the Pratt Foundation, for their commitment to engaging Australians in this complex and contested part of our national story.

In developing this exhibition, the Library has reached out to First Nations communities on the east coast of Australia and the Pacific. By listening respectfully to many voices, we hope to enhance and build our own understanding of our Cook collections and—even more importantly—build stronger connections with the communities whose lives those collections represent. *Cook and the Pacific* has required scholarship, soul-searching, recalibration, and reshaping to reflect both our admiration for Cook as scientist, navigator and leader, and our recognition that the lives of communities around the Pacific were changed forever after his journeys.

John Maynard (photographer, b. 1954)
Graffiti on a Recently Uncovered Vintage Advertising Sign in Newcastle 2010s
Courtesy John Maynard

'I'm Captain Cooked': Aboriginal perspectives on James Cook, 1770–2020

by John Maynard, Director Purai Global Indigenous and Diaspora Research Studies Centre

In 2020 the Australian nation will be torn between Anglo celebrations and Aboriginal mourning of James Cook's so-called discovery of Australia. In raising the British flag on Possession Island in the Torres Strait, Cook unleashed cataclysmic consequences upon Aboriginal people of the Australian continent. As an Aboriginal historian, one cannot but recognise, in the wake of this single event, the horrific impact and cultural destruction that would explode across the continent in the decades ahead. At its height, the Aboriginal population would teeter on near complete annihilation through disease, warfare and severe government policies. I recognise that it would be completely unrealistic to think that we would have remained immune to outside invasion and its impact even if James Cook had not stepped ashore in 1770.

In this essay, I will undertake to provide an Aboriginal perspective on Cook that examines the complexities and contradictions of the man and his interactions with Aboriginal Australia, and the impact he has had. While there has been much written about Aboriginal stories, songs, humour and derision of Cook in remote Australia, this chapter will focus on how James Cook has been remembered in south-eastern Australia. The symbolic use of James Cook by Aboriginal people is widely evident; when Ray Rose, an Aboriginal Elder originally from Dirranbandi in south-western Queensland, was asked about his health after suffering a stroke, he responded, 'Naw, not too good, I'm Captain Cooked'.

Divisions within Australia over differing viewpoints on the navigator James Cook have already begun to erupt over historical memory and its accuracy. In a recent article, Aboriginal journalist Stan Grant noted the divisive fractures within the United States over the commemoration of Southern leaders of the Civil War period and demands that the memorials be pulled down. After a walk through Hyde Park in Sydney, Grant drew attention to similar statues in Australia. He noted the monument dedicated to James Cook and its inaccuracy in stating that Cook had discovered Australia. Grant had no idea that his comment would incite such a backlash of heated opposition. He was not calling for the statue to be torn down, nor suggesting that Cook's memory should be devalued. Grant simply asked for an amendment to be made on the plaque to recognise what is now scientifically recognised as over 65,000 years of Aboriginal connection to the continent. Grant recognised that Cook was not simply 'a figure cast in bronze—a statue—but the man James Cook; a man of doubt and fear and perseverance and undoubted courage'.[1]

I am, like Grant, an admirer of James Cook as a skilled navigator and an inspiring leader of his crews. Cook's working-class upbringing instilled in him a capacity to view the world through a different lens, and he was instrumental in fostering loyalty in the crews that sailed under him. In 2014 I went on board the *Endeavour* replica at the Australian National Maritime Museum at Darling Harbour. I was struck by what an achievement it was to sail such a tiny craft across such a vast distance and through some terrifying seas. But what of his journey to Botany Bay and his orders in relation to Aboriginal people? Cook had received secret instructions from the British Admiralty, and as such from the Crown itself, which advised that in the event he found the continent, he should chart its coasts, obtain information about its people, cultivate their friendship and alliance, and appropriate any convenient trading posts in the King's name.[2] But clearly Cook did not open up any meaningful dialogue or discussion, nor did he gain any consent in claiming the entire east coast of the continent. As such he was in direct violation of his orders from the Crown. In fact, the evidence that can be gleaned from his own records clearly implies the opposite: as Cook sets down in his journal, 'all [the Aboriginal people] seem'd to want was for us to be gone'.[3] There was no welcome mat of consent rolled out. The arrogance of Cook's actions in claiming possession of the continent without any alliance with, or consent from, the owners, and the ignorance on his part that this suggests, stands in stark contrast to his glowing written record which speaks of a paradise of equality:

> [I]n reality they are far more happier than we Europeans; being wholy unacquainted not only with the superfluous but the necessary conveniencies so much sought after in Europe, they are happy in not knowing the use of them. They live in a Tranquillity which is not disturb'd by the Inequality of Condition: The Earth and sea of their own accord furnishes them with all things necessary for life … they live in a warm and fine Climate and enjoy a very wholsome Air.[4]

Cook and his impact upon Aboriginal Australia has been widely incorporated into Aboriginal songs, stories and understandings in the aftermath of 1770. Anthropologist

Additional Instructions for Lt James Cook Appointed to Command His Majts Bark the Endeavour (Secret) 30 July 1768 in Cook's Voyage 1768–1771: Copies of Correspondence Manuscripts Collection, National Library of Australia, Canberra, MS 2

Deborah Bird Rose, Japanese historian Minoru Hokari and, even more recently, the celebrated author Peter Carey are just a few who have drawn attention to the residual Aboriginal memory of James Cook.[5] These accounts feature Aboriginal people in northern and remote Australia stating that James Cook had visited their communities and had been shooting people, raping their women and taking the land. Cook's impact was clearly far-reaching, and its memory persistent. Of course, we know that he did not visit Central Australia or the Kimberley, but this recognition illustrates how deeply the event has been burned into Aboriginal consciousness.

But it is not just Central Australia and the Kimberley where Cook's memory has resonated so powerfully, and continues to do so. Communities in south-eastern Australia, where Cook most certainly did have a direct impact, have maintained and built Cook into their understandings of the past and everyday language. Sandy Cameron, a Yagirr Elder on the north coast of New South Wales, was interviewed by linguist Terry Crowley in 1973 and recorded a song in language of Cook's visit. Cameron explained:

> I told this fellow there was this Captain Cook. He was the King of the tribe and had all this tin stuff and plonk and tobacco. All the dark people had a look. He's a wuyirribin … wuyirribin that's a boat … That's a ship coming in … and they say warrayi who this ship coming in? And Captain Cook shouldn't have bowed the boat with the bush … just as much to say he's a friend, friend coming in. He jumped in a little boat … when he paddled in, he left the big boat outside … big sailing you know? Walked in waving, the chief of the tribe went to them with boomerang and spears. No … he said wanha, wanha STOP.
>
> Chief said I'll stop all of them with the spear and the boomerang. Made friends, givem tobacco and clay pipe. You don't buy them anymore. Penny each one time, shilling a dozen. And fed alright, shook hands made friends. And they was there… and this is a song I made up myself.[6]

Sandy Cameron then broke into a song, in lingo, about Cook and his coming ashore. In stating firmly that 'Captain Cook shouldn't have bowed the boat with the bush' and that the old chief had called out 'No … wanha, wanha STOP', the message conveyed is that Cook and his crew initially should not have come ashore.

The Yuin people on the south coast of New South Wales retained oral memories that recognise the lack of any formal consent or contact with Cook: 'Cook's maps were very good, but they did not show us our names for

THE LANDING OF CAPTAIN COOK AT BOTANY BAY 1770

AUSTRALIA

places. He didn't ask us.'[7] Aboriginal people across New South Wales derisively sung songs lampooning James Cook. In Armidale, they converted a young children's school rhyming song into their own dirty ditty:

> *Captain Cook chased a chook all around Australia*
> *He slipped on a rock*
> *And split his cock-a-doodle-dandy.*[8]

Similar songs were sung at the Karuah mission near Port Stephens. Good friend Ray Kelly informed me that as a kid on 'the Mish' at Armidale he knew older people who when they spotted a welfare officer, or even an unknown 'Gubba', would say, 'Lookey, lookey, here comes Cookey'.[9] The humour and retained bitter memory of James Cook, and what he represents, remain etched deeply within the fabric of many Aboriginal communities on the east coast of Australia. Cook is still at the top of the heap of historical bogeymen. As I have stated elsewhere, Cook 'transcends time and space to wreak havoc across the continent upon the Aboriginal inhabitants over the course of the past 250 years'.[10]

Whether he deserves this monster mantle is open to conjecture and challenge from wider non-Indigenous Australia, but from an Aboriginal perspective Cook remains the scapegoat for white invasion.

Percy Trompf (1902–1964)
The Landing of Captain Cook at Botany Bay 1770 1929–30
Melbourne: Australian National Travel Association
Pictures Collection, National Library of Australia, Canberra,
PIC Poster Drawer 218
Courtesy Percy Trompf Artistic Trust and Josef Lebovic Gallery Sydney

M-TUFFERY

Michel Tuffery (b. 1966)
Cookie in Te Wai Pounamu Meets Cook Strait 2011
Courtesy of the artist and Andrew Baker Art Dealer, Brisbane

Cook and the Pacific

by Susannah Helman and Martin Woods,
Exhibition Curators

There are many parts to navigator James Cook (1728–1779), and his legacy is a complex one. His navigational and scientific achievements over the course of his life were extraordinary. His three Pacific voyages, undertaken between 1768 and 1780, took him and those who sailed with him, in Cook's own words, 'farther than any other man'.[1] Cook completed the map of New Zealand and charted the east coast of Australia; he proved the imagined Great South Land did not exist and searched for the fabled Northwest Passage to Asia. As revealed in his own journals and those of his compatriots, many of which are presented here for the first time in Australia, his expeditions documented and collected flora and fauna, as well as cultural objects unknown to Europeans.

But there is another dimension to Cook's voyages. They brought the Pacific to Europe and brought Europe to the Pacific. Neither was ever the same again. These voyages represent a key moment in history, when peoples previously unknown to each other came into contact for the first time, creating opportunities for the exchange of culture, knowledge and worldviews, but also bringing the potential for confrontation.

Today, Cook remains a complex, almost mythic figure, who for many First Nations peoples across the Pacific symbolises centuries of dispossession. *Cook and the Pacific* highlights the great navigator's achievements, but it also seeks to give centre stage to the voices of those most profoundly affected by his deeds.

Despite its rich Cook collections, the National Library of Australia has never mounted a full-scale international exhibition about Captain Cook. This exhibition is a timely opportunity to reassess Cook's legacy, 250 years after his first Pacific voyage set sail from England, by revisiting stories, works of art and objects associated with the man and his voyages, and those created decades and centuries later in response to his continuing influence.

The exhibition treats Cook's voyages geographically; the many places he visited are windows onto encounters which were two-sided and often ambiguous. At times, we may be charmed by acts of collaboration, or intrigued by the exchange of gifts and favours between Pacific

Cook's Box of Instruments c. 1750
Rex Nan Kivell Collection (Pictures),
National Library of Australia, Canberra,
PIC Object Drawer 15 #A40008304

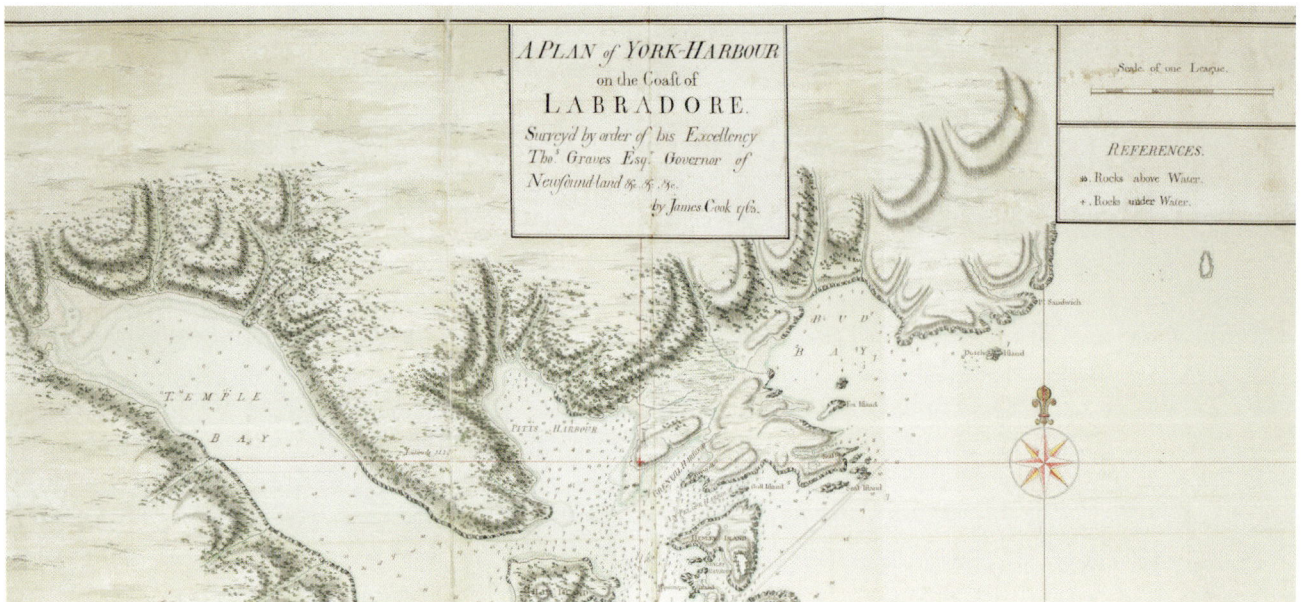

A PLAN of YORK-HARBOUR on the Coast of LABRADORE. Surveyd by order of his Excellency Thos Graves Esqr Governor of Newfoundland &c &c &c. by James Cook 1765

people and Europeans; at other times, mystified by the mistakes and miscommunications or dismayed at the consequences of actions, knowing or otherwise. Here there is space to hear First Nations voices, which are often overlooked in the historical record.

And that historical record is vast. The men on Cook's voyages documented what they saw and thought, and they collected many and varied things. They tried to map the plants and animals onto the Linnaean system of classification they knew and made comparisons between the people they met, and between the languages they heard and recorded. The reactions of Indigenous peoples to Cook were no less present in oral tradition, and over the last 250 years people have continued to reflect on and respond to these voyages. The records made on Cook's voyages, both documentary and visual, are an invaluable resource for many First Nations peoples today who wish to learn about their ancestors; they serve to complement oral traditions. Objects collected on Cook's voyages reflect many traditions that differ from region to region, and they have ongoing relevance in the places they were made. Like the living languages recorded by Cook and his men, the exhibition provides a glimpse into a much wider cultural landscape.

Just as our perspectives on Cook are complex, so too Cook the man is an enigma. Born into a large working family in rural east Yorkshire, he navigated an unorthodox path from the Whitby coal trade to

'mature-age' entrant into the navy. As his earliest maps of British expansion into Canada reveal, Cook was a brilliant practical geographer. He also came to be a capable manager of men, and perseverance is often cited as his most defining characteristic. Cook was both a product of Enlightenment ideas and a servant of a rising maritime power, forces that were at times at odds. Over three epic voyages, Cook was driven to go yet further, sowing the seeds of his demise.

Pacific encounters

London's Royal Society proposed the *Endeavour* voyage of 1768–71 to observe the transit of Venus at Tahiti of 3 June 1769. It was one of several expeditions sponsored by the Society in order to record the transit from different parts of the world. *Endeavour's* commander, James Cook, was one of the official observers at Tahiti, along with astronomer Charles Green. The results would be used to calculate the mean distance between the Earth and Venus, and consequently between the Earth and the Sun (the astronomical unit), and thus the scale of the entire solar system. Captain Samuel Wallis, just returned from his *Dolphin* voyage (1766–68), had visited Tahiti in 1767; he and his men were the first documented Europeans to do so, and he recommended it as a suitable place for observing the transit.

Over the course of Cook's three Pacific voyages, interactions and familiarity with the peoples of the Pacific led the Europeans to feel increased confidence, and perhaps overconfidence, about their ability to understand them. Society Islanders joined the voyages, most famously the Ra'iatean high priest and navigator Tupaia on the *Endeavour* voyage and Omai (or more

James Cook (1728–1779)
A Plan of York–Harbour on the Coast of Labradore Survey'd by Order of His Excellency Thos Graves Esqr Governor of Newfound-land 1763
British Library, London, Add MS 31360, f.24r
© British Library Board

6

properly, Mai) on the second voyage. Tupaia was a *tahu'a*, a priest with spiritual power grounded in navigation who remained with the voyage until his death in December 1770. During the first voyage, Europeans and Society Islanders spent several months together, and studies of island life by shipboard artists presented an idyllic picture of the South Seas. Customs and rituals were observed and documented; for example, tattooing and funerary ceremonies. Yet the Europeans struggled to understand how their political and social life was organised, and the central role that spiritual power played in its complex political and cultural relationships.

Until Cook's first Pacific voyage, the only European knowledge of Aotearoa (New Zealand) had derived from Abel Tasman, who explored parts of the North and South Islands in 1642. Cook's landing at Poverty Bay in October 1769 resulted in the deaths of several Maori, despite Tupaia's presence as interpreter and intermediary. Maori weapons and other artefacts collected by Cook revealed a sophisticated culture, and he came to respect Maori during his several visits there. The first inhabitants of New Zealand developed a distinctive oral tradition, and the documents from Cook's voyages are a valuable source for studying Maori culture. His first voyage

surveyed and circumnavigated both islands, producing the map we know today. The way was opened up for European trade and settlement, but also for the wrongs Maori have suffered since Cook's arrival.

On 31 March 1770 Cook left New Zealand to return to Britain, having recorded the transit of Venus and Polynesian island cultures. The secret instructions signed by the Lords of the Admiralty on 30 July 1768 required him to search for the supposed Great South Land, and the men of the *Endeavour* first saw the east coast of Australia, knowing it was New Holland, in April 1770. The existence of peoples in the southern hemisphere had been part of European tradition since the old Ptolemaic notion of a land-locked Indian Ocean. In this context, Cook's Pacific voyages were part of a continuing project

LEFT

*Miniature Celestial Globe Reputed to Have Been Used by
Captain Cook* 1765
Pictures Collection, State Library Victoria, Melbourne, H5088

RIGHT

Philippe Jacques de Loutherbourg (1740–1812)
Chief Mourner Otahaite (*Costume Design for the Pantomime 'Omai'*) 1785
Pictures Collection, National Library of Australia, Canberra,
PIC Solander Box A67 #R145

Monday 30th. As soon as the wooders and waterers were come on board to dinner 10 or 12 of the natives came to the watering place and took away their canoes that lay there but did not offer to touch any one of our casks that had been left ashore and in the after noon 16 or 18 of them came boldly up to within 100 yards of our people at the watering place and there made a stand. Mr Hicks who was the officer ashore did all in his power to intice them to him by offering them presents &c. but it was to no purpose all they seem'd to want was for us to be gone after

of refining both global geography and the science of navigation.

His encounter with mainland Australia, first marked on maps at Point Hicks in eastern Victoria, and then north along the coast of New South Wales and Queensland all the way to Torres Strait, was instrumental not only in a revolution in botanical, zoological and other European sciences, but also in transforming places of Indigenous spiritual and social significance into place names for later exploration and occupation. On the New South Wales south coast, Gulaga (Mount Dromedary) and Didthul (Pigeon House Mountain) were among the distinctive features seen and recorded from the *Endeavour* that were of primary significance to the Yuin peoples.

For more than six months, the expedition followed the coastline north, for the most part disembarking only briefly to source fresh water and food. There was little interaction with the local peoples or understanding formed of their way of life. Yet the consequences of the reports Cook and his colleagues made to the British government were great. Joseph Banks recommended Botany Bay as a site for a penal colony, assuring the government that the local people would give little trouble. The Aboriginal peoples met on the *Endeavour* voyage were not particularly interested in the goods the Europeans had to offer, and unlike many of the other First Nations people met, they would rarely trade. Cook and Banks both remarked on this with some admiration, Cook noting that they 'seem'd to set no Value upon any thing we gave them, nor would they ever part with any thing of their own for any one article we could offer them; this, in my opinion argues that they think themselves provided with all the necessarys of Life and that they have no superfluities'.[2] The journals of Cook, Banks and Richard Pickersgill (master's mate on the *Endeavour*) record numerous campfires seen as they travelled up the coast. At Botany Bay, where they stayed for eight days and nights from late April to early May 1770, interactions were characterised by avoidance and resistance on the part of the local peoples, and by a British resort to firearms. In his journal on 30 April, Cook noted 'all they seem'd to want was for us to be gone'.[3]

Interactions were more sustained at Waalumbaal Birri (Endeavour River), where the voyage remained for 48 days carrying out repairs after crashing into the Great Barrier Reef in June 1770. Records of a disagreement about turtles, a gesture of coming together on the part of an old Guugu Yimithirr man, and an extensive wordlist attest to genuine engagement.

By the time the *Endeavour* hit the reef near what is now Endeavour River, it was heavily laden with specimens, and cultural objects collected on the voyage. Six of its ten cannon, as well as pig iron and stone ballast, were jettisoned so that it could be hauled off. In 1969 the Academy of Natural Sciences of Philadelphia funded an expedition to find these, using the new technology of a magnetometer, as coral growth had obscured them. The wreck of the *Endeavour* itself is thought to rest in Newport's outer harbour off Rhode Island, USA, where it was scuttled in 1778.

The *Endeavour* voyage's documenting and collecting of the natural world at both Botany Bay and Endeavour River were extensive. An immense number of botanical specimens collected by Joseph Banks and Daniel Solander were preserved and described, to be drawn by Sydney Parkinson. Most of the watercolours of Australian plants were completed in London by other artists. Copperplates were engraved, but the project was abandoned. The animals the visitors saw puzzled them. In his journal entry for 25 June 1770, Banks records seeing a kangaroo. 'In gathering plants today I myself had the good fortune to see the beast so much talkd of, tho but imperfectly; he was not only like a grey hound in size and running but had a long tail … what to liken him to I could not tell, nothing certainly that I have seen at all resembles him.'[4] Australian birds, with the exception of pigeons, were found to be too smart to trap easily.

At Possession Island, following a running survey of Australia's east coast, *Cook* claimed it for George III, an event simply recorded in the official log: 'at 6 Possession was taken of this Country in his majesty's Name & under his Coulours Fired several volleys of small arms on the occasion & Cheer'd 3 times which was answerd from the ship'.[5] At various points during the mapping of New Zealand, Cook claimed various lands for the King, and he followed the same pattern as the Australian survey proceeded, though, it must be said, with more haste. After nearly three years at sea the priority was a swift return voyage. The secret additional instructions—which

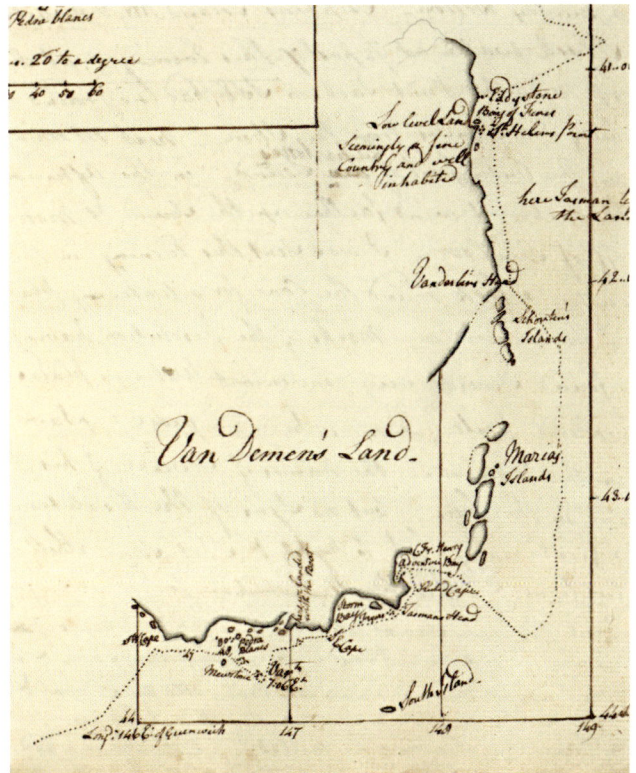

he was ordered to 'carry into execution' after observing the transit of Venus—had given opaque direction about how the taking possession of land on the voyage, after Tahiti, should occur. Should he find the 'Great South Land' inhabited, he was to take possession of the country 'with the Consent of the Natives'. No mention is made in the instructions of New Holland, though it was known from Tasman's voyage of 1642–43, and Cook was aware when he encountered land near Point Hicks, almost due north of where the Dutch had left Tasmania, that he had reached its eastern limit. The instructions go on to say what he should do if he did not find the continent: 'You will also observe with accuracy the Situation of such Islands as you may discover in the Course of your Voyage that have not hitherto been discover'd by Europeans & take Possession for His Maj[esty].'[6] Though no consent had been obtained from Indigenous Australians, Cook the navigator was politically savvy enough to appreciate that having surveyed over 2,000 miles (3,200 kilometres) of new coast, raising the colours was obligatory, particularly in light of the emerging French interest in the Pacific. Whatever the reasoning, Cook effectively added the name 'New South Wales' to the world map.

Voyaging between worlds

It is not so well known that Cook's ships visited Australia on all three Pacific voyages, the latter two of which to Van Diemen's Land (now Tasmania) are naturally overshadowed by the *Endeavour's* voyage up the east coast of the mainland. Cook himself did not reach Van Diemen's Land until 1777, on his third and final Pacific voyage. The expedition, mounted to search for the Northwest Passage and to return Mai to his home on Huahine in the Society Islands, visited New Zealand, the Cook Islands and Tonga, before reaching Hawaii early in 1778.

Europeans had not visited Hawaii before Cook did so in 1778, and he soon realised that the islanders were part of an impressive diaspora of seafaring cultures. He and his men admired their intricate *kapa* (barkcloth) and their headdresses and capes adorned with red and yellow bird feathers. They observed the plants and animals that thrived on the islands, and recognised the ingenuity, skill and art with which the Hawaiians used the resources available to them. It seemed a lifestyle characterised by abundance, spirituality and ample leisure. They were surprised to catch the sound of Society Islands words in their speech, and on asking for hogs, breadfruit, yams, and so on, they found they were understood.

In the month Cook spent in the Hawaiian islands (which he named Sandwich Islands, in honour of the First Lord of the Admiralty, John Montagu, 4th Earl of Sandwich), the voyagers bartered for goods and engaged in some social interaction, though Cook tried to prohibit contact between his men and the women, to reduce the spread of venereal diseases.

Cook returned to Hawaii almost a year later, after extensive exploration of the west coast of North America and the Siberian coast. Fatefully, he had arrived in the season of *makahiki*, which ran from October to February. The god of this season was *Lono makua* (Father Lono), a season of abundance, when celebrations were the norm, and the rival Hawaiian island kingdoms were forbidden from engaging in warfare. After Cook's vessels anchored in Kealakekua Bay (on the Kona coast of the island of Hawaii) on 17 January, he was welcomed and honoured as a chief of goodwill. Gifts were exchanged, and for a time Cook and his men enjoyed the hospitality of the island's royal family. In early February the ships departed, on good terms though having tested the patience of Kalani'ōpu'u, the *Ali'i nui* (king) of Kona and other districts. Within days of departing, a storm forced their return for repairs. This time there was no welcome. As he had on other occasions, Cook misread Hawaiian attitudes to trade, and a series of minor incidents culminated in the theft of the *Discovery's* cutter. Cook went ashore with some officers and marines and attempted to take Kalani'ōpu'u hostage. In the ensuing melee, four marines, Cook and several Hawaiians were killed.

The Bernice Pauahi Bishop Museum in Honolulu holds a swordfish dagger which has claims to having been that used in Cook's death. Cook's voyages subsequently brought European attention to these islands and the diseases that devastated the population.

Cook visited the islands of Tonga on three occasions on his second and third voyages. Tonga was given the name 'Friendly Islands', owing to the apparently cordial relationship between the Europeans and several island chiefs. Paintings by artist John Webber of canoes and other scenes invariably evoke harmony, and on his third voyage Cook himself presented a red cloth to the *Tamaha* (daughter of the sister of the *Tu'i Tonga* or king). Yet such impressions belied deeper currents. Like his predecessors Tasman and Wallis, Cook did not comprehend the complex Tongan family ranking system, though he did admire Tongan canoes for their speed and manoeuvrability. Unlike others completed elsewhere, the skilful portraits executed by William Hodges, the artist on Cook's second Pacific voyage, during fleeting visits to Rapa Nui (Easter Island) and New Caledonia reflected little cultural exchange. Similarly, impressions of the parts of the Marquesas Islands visited on Cook's second voyage were superficial, though the expedition's written and visual records are among the earliest known descriptions of these societies.

The voyages' journals describe many situations in which Pacific island peoples and Europeans miscommunicated, though few led to the sort of violence seen at Kealakekua Bay. Relations with the Melanesian peoples of Vanuatu (New Hebrides) were from the outset very difficult, and usually brief. The reception occasioned by the arrival of the *Resolution* at Port Resolution (on the south-eastern corner of the island) in August 1774 was at best lukewarm. Hodges' portrait of a man of the island of Tanna possibly depicted Paowang, who became friendly and was entertained aboard the ship.

After the trials of the first two Pacific voyages, Cook was tired yet unready to reconcile himself to a life of retirement. By all accounts, he required little persuasion to lead the Admiralty's quest to unravel the mystery of whether there was a Northwest Passage between the Atlantic and the Pacific, a longed-for timesaver for European traders. Cook's endeavours in the North Pacific have been relatively overlooked in Cook studies. Although it was just as ambitious an expedition as the earlier two, the third voyage has usually been overshadowed by Cook's death. Major achievements include a contribution to the task of making better maps of the North Pacific and visual records of the way of life of the local peoples (in particular, at Prince William

Sound and Nootka Sound), the work of the prolific artists John Webber and William Ellis.

After Cook's death, the *Discovery* and *Resolution* sailed southward, following the Asian coast from Kamchatka. They stopped at Macao, Vietnam (Pulo Condore) and Indonesia (Cracatoa). All these regions were well known to Europeans, yet Webber and Ellis continued their accustomed documentation of people met and views seen.

Navigating the Pacific

Webber and the other artists also depicted a variety of Polynesian, North American and Australian Indigenous craft, capturing something of the technology, observation and lore behind wayfinding techniques and canoe construction methods. Polynesian navigators (and those of other Austronesian cultures) employed a range of techniques, based on their understanding of the stars, of the movement of ocean currents and wave patterns, of the air and sea interference patterns caused by islands and atolls, of the flight of birds, of the winds and the weather more generally. And, as Tupaia's map (centred on his home island of Ra'iatea) shows, they relied also on a knowledge of the geography of the Pacific.

In many ways, Indigenous Pacific navigation may be contrasted with European methods. As Cook experienced it at first hand, this was non-instrument navigation, conducted without the aid of compass, sextant or clocks. He was never persuaded of its superiority, though he could value its usefulness. Yet like their European counterparts, Polynesian methods could be adapted to suit long-distance voyaging. Double-hulled canoes were more stable than single-hulled outrigger canoes and had greater carrying capacity (in terms of supplies and people). Development of the shape of the sail and the rig that supports it allowed canoes to reach (sail nearly towards the direction from which the wind comes), while open-ocean voyaging relied on studying the position and movement of celestial bodies.

The Cook voyages are remarkable for the exclusive use of colliers, coal ships produced in the north Yorkshire port town Whitby. Broad and sturdy with a large internal capacity, *Endeavour* was classed as a bark by the navy, which was ideal in shallow waters and could be readily beached to carry out repairs. The ship's ocean-going qualities were doubted by some, but Cook and those who had worked on these colliers on the northern seas were confident that, with modifications, *Endeavour* would acquit itself over longer voyages. Much of this was to do with sheathing the hull against ship-worm, and the division of its 'tween decks for extra cabin space to allow

for Banks and other scientists. On his second voyage he sailed in *Resolution* accompanied by *Adventure*, and on the third, once more in *Resolution*, this time accompanied by *Discovery*.

Frequently depicted by the voyage artists, *Resolution* impressed Cook greatly, who thought it perfectly fit for purpose. It nearly wasn't so. Joseph Banks had intended to sail again with Cook and proposed modifications, including an additional upper deck to allow for a larger scientific entourage. The additions were removed when it was realised that they made the ship top-heavy. Banks withdrew from the voyage and redirected his energies towards a trip to Iceland.

The eighteenth century saw major improvements in publications and tools for navigators. France and Britain established governmental hydrographic or surveying offices whose charts and sailing directions were regularly corrected and republished. The 1767 publication of the first *Nautical Almanac and Astronomical Ephemeris* by the Astronomer Royal, Nevil Maskelyne, provided tables of lunar distances to aid in calculating longitude. The method required accurate daily measurements of the angle between the moon and known stars, essential for 'great circle sailing' (the shortest distance between two points on a globe). The navigator had at his disposal a reflecting octant or quadrant (predecessors of the modern sextant) for measuring the altitude of the sun and for taking star sights. As the voyage progressed, these and other tools aided in accurate coastal surveying, and in the creation of reliable maps.

Even with Maskelyne's *Nautical Almanac*, accurate determination of longitude remained a challenge to navigation. Rival instrument makers took up the challenge set by the British government's Board of Longitude, and chronometers designed as a means of keeping accurate time during the voyage were tested by Cook on his second Pacific voyage. The idea was to set the chronometer to the time at the prime meridian (Greenwich), while local noon would be established by the sun. The difference in times translates to longitude. Cook carried instruments by London watchmakers Larcum Kendall and John Arnold. Kendall's 'K1', a copy of John Harrison's 'H4', carried aboard the *Resolution* proved reliable throughout the voyage, and compared closely to measurements calculated using Maskelyne's lunar tables. Cook took three timepieces with him made by Arnold—two for his companion ship, *Adventure*, and one for the *Resolution*. None of the Arnold timekeepers was as reliable as K1. Kendall's and Arnold's clocks later inspired part of Australian poet Kenneth Slessor's 'Five visions of Captain Cook' (1931).

Evidence suggests Cook's ships carried more extensive reference libraries than might be expected given the confined, limited and multipurpose spaces. Shipboard journals prove that the works they contained were in regular use. We know most about the library of the *Endeavour*. Voyages such as these were reliant on the maps and accounts of those who had preceded them. Navigators needed to be aware of what had already been written about and mapped. If they wanted to contribute to that literature, publication of a voyage account with maps, portraits and views was the major way to do that. Cook records his exasperation on the third voyage when he realised that he had no reliable map of the north but was carrying instead Jacob von Staehlin's map of 1773–74 that showed Alaska as an island.

Cook after Cook

The question of how to interpret the Cook voyages began during James Cook's lifetime. Indeed, he was an active participant, objecting strenuously to the officially sanctioned account of the *Endeavour* voyage journals that was published in 1773. Written by a journalist named John Hawkesworth, this publication was ostensibly 'drawn up from the journals', but took great liberties with Cook's text.[7] Hawkesworth later claimed that Cook had seen the text in draft form. News of the animals collected and botany seen on the *Endeavour* voyage led to a decades-long enterprise to interpret, classify and document, and, in the case of botanical specimens, reproduce for publication (something only fully achieved in the 1980s). All naval journals were required to be submitted to the Admiralty at the end of the voyage, but this did not account for draft and other copies, and those that were surreptitiously kept. On subsequent voyages, Cook was aware that his journals would be published, and after the second voyage he was given time to write up his journal. In the years that followed Cook's death, accounts by his scientists, artists, officers and crew jostled with dramatised works in a market keen to know about the voyages, and as far as Britons were concerned, to share in the glory. The Admiralty sought to stifle accounts that would steal the thunder of the official account. A famous case in point is the example of Johann Reinhold Forster, naturalist on the second Pacific voyage, whose desire to publish his own account was thwarted, though not entirely defeated.

News of Cook's death ricocheted, eventually, around the world. A letter details the reaction of Catherine the Great of Russia. The British ambassador at St Petersburg, Sir James Harris, reported that 'she was greatly

concern'd' to hear of his 'untimely death'.[8] A more subtle marker is an unfinished tapa waistcoat embroidered by Cook's wife, Elizabeth, her work perhaps interrupted by the news. Cook may have commissioned it from her, intending to wear it at Court. Elizabeth Cook became the guardian of much that her husband had owned— including drafts and copies of maps and journals—and is known to have retained, distributed and also destroyed much over the decades of a long widowhood.

Publishing a record of a voyage was the way to ensure a contribution to knowledge. After the death of Cook, and also that of his deputy, Charles Clerke, the task fell primarily to James King, who returned to England as captain of the *Discovery*, Canon John Douglas, who edited the text, and Joseph Banks, who oversaw the production of the volumes. Maps had to be printed, and works of art catalogued, selected and readied for engraving. Proof plates show the stages involved in engraving, and correspondence reveals how complicated a task it was. The last official Cook voyage account finally appeared in 1784.

Many of those who sailed with Cook kept their own collections for the information of their families— officers John Elliott and John Gore, for example. Elliott kept works of art completed at sea and wrote a memoir. Gore, who sailed on four Pacific voyages, including Cook's first and third Pacific voyages, kept his Dollond telescope. There was no obligatory repository for objects and specimens, as there was for written accounts. The fledgling British Museum, the private Leverian Museum, patrons such as Lord Sandwich, collectors such as Joseph Banks, surgeon John Hunter and the naturalist Thomas Pennant and others, were all obvious destinations for such collections.

In the mid- to late 1780s, the Cook voyages were still topical in London. The second Pacific voyage had brought the Ra'iatean man Mai to England. He had been much fêted in London between 1774 and 1776 and taking him home was important to Cook on the third Pacific voyage. Mai was remembered in London the following decade when the extravagant production, designed by Alsatian Philippe Jacques de Loutherbourg, in collaboration with John Webber, was launched at the Theatre Royal, Covent Garden, in December 1785. De Loutherbourg's costume, set and prop designs drew on objects collected on the voyages and on the portraits done from life by John Webber. The production did much to mythologise Cook's voyages, and culminated in a giant scene depicting the apotheosis of Captain Cook, thereby placing Cook in the company of James I,

famously shown ascending to the heavens in the work by Peter Paul Rubens that adorns the ceiling of the Banqueting House in London's Whitehall.

The Cook voyages remained a key moment in exploration history and Cook a revered figure in the pantheon of British heroes and explorers well into the twentieth century. Cook was respected for his skills as an explorer and surveyor, his handling of officers and men and his attention to health on board his ships. Long after his death, navies and sailors were still using his surveys. Yet there has long been uneasiness about the voyages, even in the British accounts. The potential effects of the European contact with the peoples of the Pacific were remarked upon by scientists, and even by Cook himself. Yet little published criticism of Cook emerged until late in the twentieth century. Celebrations to mark the formation of the Commonwealth of Australia in 1901 included an event at Botany Bay, followed by the erection of Cook monuments and the widespread belief that Captain Cook 'discovered' Australia. The authoritative edition of Cook's journals by New Zealand historian J.C. Beaglehole preceded a bicentenary of the Australian landing in 1770 that was outwardly positive, despite the recognition in the work of scholars such as Beaglehole himself, the art historian Bernard Smith and others that there was a more nuanced story to be told.[9]

Reactions and responses to Cook have changed over the centuries, and in Australian life little else has been as vocal, emotional and imaginative as Aboriginal and Torres Strait Islander responses to Cook. The navigator has come to symbolise centuries of violence and dispossession suffered by the First Nations people of Australia. By the 1970 bicentenary of Cook's voyage up the east coast, protests were gathering strength.

The poet Kath Walker (Oodgeroo Noonuccal) was involved in these through her role as Queensland State Secretary of the Federal Council for the Advancement of Aborigines and Torres Strait Islanders. Walker told *The Australian* that a silent protest of Aboriginal people wearing black would follow the Queen, who was to visit in March and April 1970. Referring to the consequences of Cook's voyages for Aboriginal and Torres Strait Islander Australians, particularly Tasmanians, she said, 'We who are left will mourn their death as well as the way in which we live now, as second-class citizens. We intend a silent, dignified vigil of protest. Those who cannot afford to wear black clothes will be asked to wear black arm bands or bows.'[10] The legacy of Cook was again a focus around the 1988 bicentenary commemorations; for example, in the 'We have survived' series of posters produced by the Northern Land Council and the Central Land Council. In the 1992 Mabo decision the High Court of Australia recognised Indigenous land rights. Artists such as Tony Albert, Gordon Bennett, Daniel Boyd, Michael Cook, Karla Dickens, Christian Thompson and Jason Wing challenge and reinterpret assumptions that are widely held about Cook, cementing his curiously central role in the Australian psyche.

One of the challenges posed by the Library's collections—but also one of its strengths—is how in its richness it can trace the changes in perception about Cook and his legacy.

Karla Dickens (b. 1967)
'The nips are getting bigger/I'd better go get somethin' harder' 2015
Courtesy of the artist and Andrew Baker Art Dealer, Brisbane

The journals kept by Captain James Cook and his fellow travellers during their three Pacific voyages are remarkable for the many records of First Nations language they contain. Most take the form of word lists, and in many instances they are the first written record of, and English translation of, Pacific languages; they are drawn from Australia, Aotearoa (New Zealand), the North Pacific, Hawaii and other islands throughout the South Pacific. They include the first written record of the word *kangaroo*, in a word list taken at Waalumbaal Birri (Endeavour River) in northern Australia, and the first written transcription of a *haka* (traditional Maori war cry), in the journal of surgeon David Samwell.

They are evidence of two groups of people coming together, both of whom are trying to make themselves understood, and understand each other. The sequence and nature of the words vary from place to place, suggesting that these were unique and evolving conversations at various meetings across the Pacific.

p. 15
A Short Vocabulary of the Guugu Yimithirr People,
Waalumbaal Birri (Endeavour River), p. 306
in Joseph Banks (1743–1820)
Endeavour Journal, 15 August 1769 – 12 July 1771
State Library of New South Wales, Sydney,
SAFE/ Banks papers/ Series 03.02

p. 16
A Vocabulary of the Language of the People of New
Holland (Guugu Yimithirr), Waalumbaal Birri
(Endeavour River), p. 149
in Sydney Parkinson (c. 1745–1771)
A Journal of a Voyage to the South Seas, in His Majesty's
Ship, the Endeavour
London: Printed for Stanfield Parkinson, 1773
Rex Nan Kivell Collection (Australian Printed)
National Library of Australia, Canberra, NK2702

p. 17
List Comparing Words from New Zealand and
South Sea Islands, ff.215r-215v
in James Cook (1728–1779)
Journal of HMB Endeavour 1768–71
Manuscripts Collection, National Library
of Australia, Canberra, MS 1
Inscribed on the UNESCO Memory of the World
Register, 2001

United Nations
Educational, Scientific and
Cultural Organization

Memory of
the World

Some account of New Holland

consists some only being added that were in only
one list such as from the ease with which signs
might be contrived to ask them were thought little
less certain then the others

Wageegee	the head.	Meanang	Fire
Morye	the hair.	Walba	a stone.
Melæa	the ears.	Yowall	Sand.
Yembe	the Lips.	Gurká	a Rope.
Bonjoo	the Nose.	Bama	a Man.
Unjar	the tongue	Poinja	a male Turtle
Wallar	the Beard	Mameingo	a female
Doomboo	the Neck	Maragan	a Canoe.
Cayo	the Nipples.	Pelenyo	to Paddle
Toolpoor	the Navel.	Takai	set down
Mangal	the Hands.	Mierbarrar	Smooth.
Coman	the thighs.	Garmbe	Blood.
Pongo	the Knees.	Yocou	Wood.
Edamal	the Feet.	Tapool	bone in nose
Kniorror	the Heel	charngala	a Bag
chumal	the Sole	cherr	Expressions
Chongarn	the ankle.	Chereo	may be of admiration which
Kulke	the Nails.	Yarcaw	they continually used while in
Gallan	the Sun	Gut tut tut tut	company with us

They very often use the article Ge which seems
to answer to our English a as Ge Gurka a rope

Morcol,	*The throat.*
Coyor,	*The breast.*
Coyoor,	*The nipples.*
Melmal,	*The pit of the stomach.*
Gippa,	*The belly.*
Toolpoor,	*The navel.*
Mocoo,	*The back.*
Eèimbar,	*The sides or ribs.*
Aco, or acol,	*The arms.*
Camor, or gamorga,	*The arm-pits.*
Mangal,	*The hands.*
Eboorbalga,	*The thumb.*
Egalbaiga,	*The three fingers next the thumb.*
Nakil, or eboornakil,	*The little finger.*
Coenjoo,	*The hips.*
Booca,	*The anus.*
Coman,	*The thighs.*
Atta,	*The ham.*
Pongo,	*The knees.*
Peegoorga,	*The legs.*
Chongarn,	*The ancle.*
Edamal,	*The feet.*
Kniororor,	*The heel.*
Chumal,	*The sole of the foot.*
Jambooingar, or tambooingar,	*The toes.*
Kolke,	*The nails.*
Pandal,	*A sore.*
Mòro,	*The scars on their bodies.*
Tennapuke, or jennapuke.	*The hole in their nostrils made for the bone ornament.*
Cotta,	*A dog.*
Kangooroo,	*The leaping quadruped.*
Taquol, or jaquol,	*An animal of the viverra kind.*

Waowa,

English	New Zeland	South-Sea Islands
A Thief ------	Amootoo -----	Teto
To Examine ---	Matakitako -----	Matactai
To Sing -----	Eheiva ----------	Heiva --
Bad ------	Keno -----	Eno
Trees ------	Oratow ------	Eraou
Grand Father --	Toubouna -----	Toubouna
No ------	Kaoura -----	Oure ---
Number 1 ----	Tahai -----	Tahai
2 ----	Rua -----	Rua
3 ---	Torou -----	Torou
4 ---	Ha ------	Heo
5 ---	Rema -----	Rema
6 ----	Ono -----	Ono
7 ---	Etu -----	Hetu
8 ----	Wharou -----	Wharou
9 ---	Toa -----	Hyva
10 ----	Angahourou ----	Ahourou
What do you call this or that	Owy Terra ----	Owy Terra

These are some small difference in the Language
spoke by the Ahei-no mouweans and those
of Tovy poe nammu but this difference seemd
to me to be only in the pronunciation and
is no more than what we find between one
part of England and another, what is here
inserted as a specimen is that spoke by the
People of Ahei no mouwe. what is meant by
the South sea Islands are those Islands we

1. WHO IS JAMES COOK AND WHERE DID HE COME FROM?

James Cook was born in a cottage in the rural Yorkshire village of Marton in 1728. A Whitby coal trader in his early career, he joined the Royal Navy and served in the Seven Years' War (1756–63), fought between Great Britain and France. He honed his marine survey and mapping skills in Nova Scotia and Newfoundland. In 1768 Cook undertook the first of three British expeditions he led into the Pacific Ocean. The voyages were partly scientific in nature, and partly strategic, positioning Britain as a power in the Pacific.

Cook's legacy is a complex one. For some he is the great navigator, a man firm and fair, and well suited to his calling. The scientific achievements revealed in these artefacts of the Cook voyages were immense: European knowledge of the Pacific world exploded and new vistas opened up. Yet each Pacific encounter was a two-sided affair, and today Cook and the impact his voyages had on First Nations across the Pacific, including Aboriginal and Torres Strait Islander Australia, continue to resonate powerfully.

John Webber (1752–1793)
Portrait of Captain James Cook RN 1782
National Portrait Gallery, Canberra, Acc. No. 2000.25
Purchased in 2000 by the Commonwealth Government with the
generous assistance of Robert Oatley AO and John Schaeffer AO

John Webber, the artist on Cook's third Pacific voyage, produced
several portraits of Cook. Completed after Cook's death, this is one
of the major oil portraits of the explorer—others are by Nathaniel
Dance and William Hodges. It shows him as a commanding figure,
far removed from his humble beginnings in the north of England.

His right hand wears a glove to disguise an old war wound, and
the left points to the artist's signature. Webber may have used this
painting to advertise his trade, capitalising on his connection to
the famous navigator. An earlier version of the portrait was given
to Tu, later Pōmare I, king of Tahiti at Matavai, who, having sat for
a portrait himself, asked Cook for one in return. That painting was
last seen by Captain George Vancouver in 1792. Another version
belonged to Cook's widow, Elizabeth, and this one was in the artist's
collection at his death.

Michael Cook (b. 1968) Bidjara Peoples
Undiscovered #4 2010
Courtesy of the artist and Andrew Baker Art Dealer, Brisbane

James Cook (1728–1779)
Navigation Notes, Canada 1758
Manuscripts Collection, National Library of Australia, Canberra,
MS 1627

As master of the *Pembroke*, Cook took part in the siege of Louisburg
and the survey of the Saint Lawrence River that led to the capture
of Quebec. The manuscript, headed 'Descriptions for Sailing in and
out of Ports with Soundings, Marks for particular Rocks, Shoals,
etc. with Latitudes, Longitudes, Tides & Variations of the compass',
describes approaches, currents and soundings taken around various
topographic features, including Flat Island, Bonaventure Island,
Cape Gaspe and Cap-des-Rosiers.

From the Birds Islands to Cape Gaspey, the North entrance of Gaspey Bay, by some called Cape Forillon, is NW ½ West distant 43 leagues —

From Birds Islands to Cape Rosier is N BW northerly distance 45 leagues.

Cape Gaspey is very remarkable, the NE side being high steep white cliffs, and close by it stands a white rock called the Old Woman; when this rock is open of the cape, and you are some distance off it appears like a sail: this cape is steep too having 5 and 6 fathom close to it and 40 fms a ¼ mile off —

Latitude 48..51 — Longitude 63..44 West Variation of the Compass 17 West

Three leagues to the Northward of Cape Gaspey is Cape Rosier, the South entrance of the River St Lawrence, it is a very low point and not easily to be distinguished unless you are very near in, but the land above it is very high and may be seen at a great distance —

Latitude 49..00 Longitude 63..45 West —

In coming from Birds Islands to Gaspey or Cape Rosier the first land you generally make is the high land over the Island of Bonaventura which may be seen 11 or 12 leagues — This Island lies about 4 or 6 leagues to the Southward of Cape Gaspey, and about two miles from the Main it is about one league in length and pretty high, and I believe bold too all round: I have been informed from undoubted authority that there is very good channel between it and the main wherein is 15, 18 and 20 fathom water. ~~~~~~~~~~~~

From the Island of Bonaventura to the Flat Island, a small low Island at the South-entrance of Gaspey Bay, is North and South, about 2 leagues; you will have 28 and 30 fathom water within 1½ mile of the Island and I believe may approach it much nearer with great safety

James Cook (1728–1779)
A Sketch of Harbour Grace and Carbonere in Newfoundland 1762
Manuscripts Collection, National Library of Australia, Canberra,
MS 5

Cook served in eastern North America from 1758 to 1767 and
kept a notebook in which he recorded observations relating to the
coastlines of Nova Scotia and Newfoundland. The notebook dates
from the conclusion of the Seven Years' War, and includes his sketch
of Harbour Grace, an important port and fishing centre on the
east coast of Newfoundland. The sketch marked the beginnings of
Cook's five-year survey of Newfoundland, an achievement largely
responsible for his being awarded command of the *Endeavour* voyage.

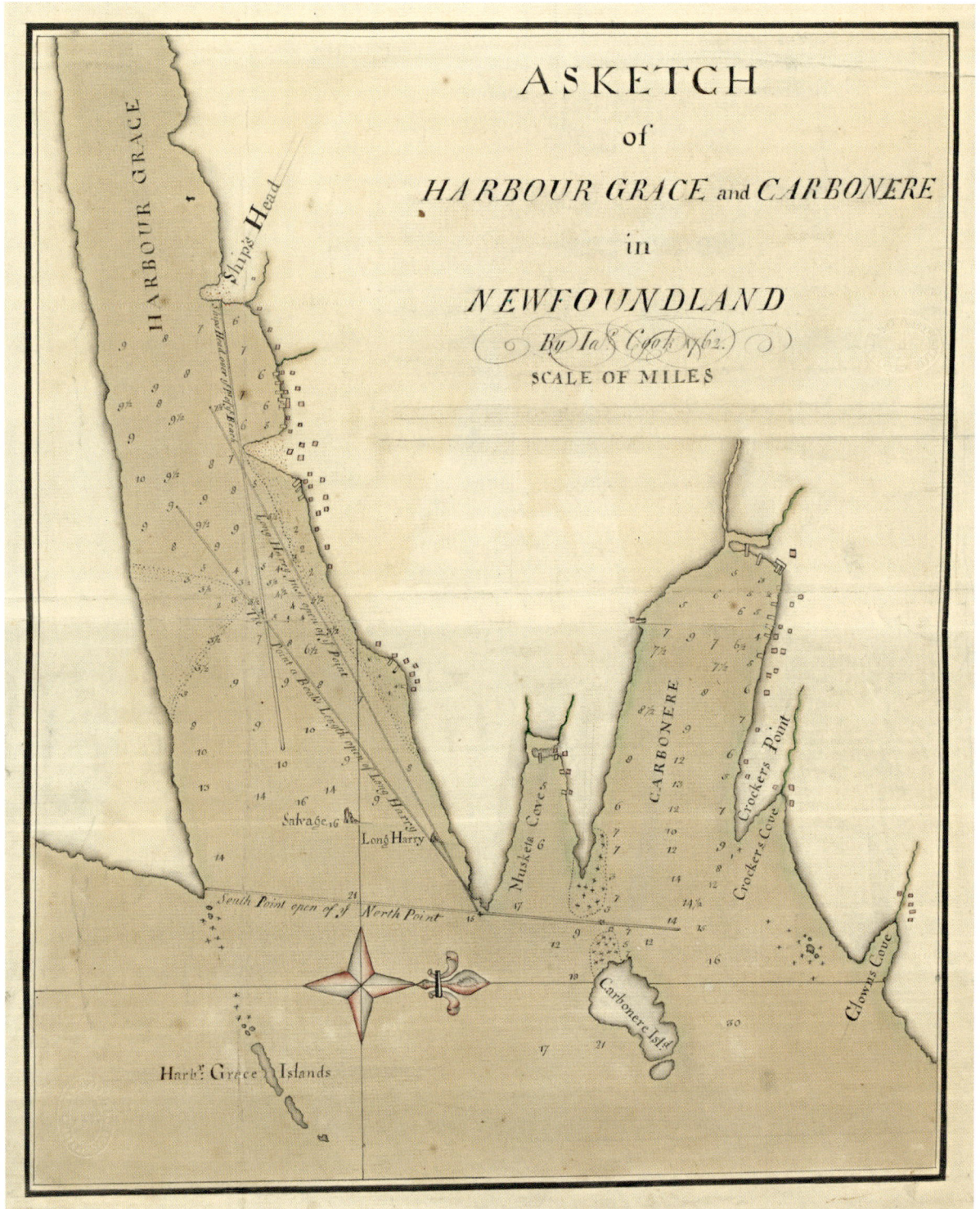

T. Pouilly (Paris)
Brass Graphometer Belonging to Captain Cook c. 1684
State Library of New South Wales, Sydney, SAFE/LR 31

The graphometer (or semicircumferentor) is a surveying instrument used for measuring angles. This instrument, believed to have been used by Cook in North America in the 1750s and 1760s, was for setting out landmarks in preliminary survey work.

Thomas Luny (1759–1837)
The Bark, Earl of Pembroke, later Endeavour, Leaving Whitby Harbour in 1768 c. 1790
Pictures Collection, National Library of Australia, Canberra, PIC Screen 98 #R3397

Cook knew Whitby well. Born in the rural Yorkshire village of Marton in 1728, he began his working life in Whitby's coal trade, before joining the Royal Navy in 1755. After honing his marine survey and mapping skills in North America, in 1768 he undertook the first of his three expeditions into the Pacific, in the *Endeavour*. Here the artist shows the former Whitby collier *Earl of Pembroke* making its way south for commissioning into the Royal Navy as HMB *Endeavour*.

Philip Stephens (1723–1809)
Letter to James Cook 11 April 1772 in *Letterbook* 1771–78
Manuscripts Collection, National Library of Australia, Canberra,
MS 6

The Europeans who visited the Pacific and its peoples were collectors, with a passion for gathering material evidence and souvenirs. The passion was mutual, and ships needed to carry things that could be traded or given. This copy of a letter from the Admiralty Office lists the 'several things' to be provided for the ships of Cook's second Pacific voyage, 'in order to be exchanged for Refreshments with the Natives of such New discovered or unfrequented Countries as they may touch at, or to be distributed to them in Presents to our Interest'. Such items included tools, looking glasses, 'Old Shirts not Patch'd', 'Hatts', 'Fine Old Sheets' and kettles, and especially iron 'Spike Nails', which provided harder, sharper points for carving, drilling or tipping weapons.

James Douglas, 14th Earl of Morton (1702–1768)
Hints Offered to the Consideration of Captain Cooke, Mr Bankes, Dr Solander and the Other Gentlemen Who Go upon the Expedition on Board the Endeavour 10 August 1768
Papers of Sir Joseph Banks (Manuscripts), National Library of Australia, Canberra, MS 9 Series 3 Item 113

Written just over a fortnight before the *Endeavour* set sail from Plymouth, this letter from Lord Morton, President of the Royal Society, provided Cook and his companions with the Society's views on how they should conduct themselves. In particular, it counselled them 'to exercise the utmost patience and forbearance' in the treatment of any inhabitants of lands visited:

> *sheding the blood of those people is a crime of the highest nature:—*
> *They are human creatures, the work of the same omnipotent Author,* equally under his care with the most polished European ... They are the natural, and in the strictest sense of the word, the legal possessors of the several Regions they inhabit. No European Nation has a right to occupy any part of their country, or settle among them without their voluntary consent.

2. NAVIGATING THE PACIFIC

When the British reached the Pacific, they found a navigational knowledge system to rival their own. Indigenous Pacific navigation employed a range of techniques including observation of the stars, ocean currents and wave effects, air and sea interference patterns caused by islands and atolls, the flight of birds, the winds and the weather. As Cook saw it at first hand, this was 'non-instrument' navigation, undertaken without the aid of a grid, compass, sextant or clocks. Even so, exponents such as Tupaia, the Ra'iatean priest and navigator who joined the *Endeavour* voyage in 1769, could direct them across the ocean from island to island.

The British had made innovations of their own. Cook's vessels were adapted North Sea coal ships: flat-bottomed, with a long box-like body and a deep hold. The design was ideal for long voyaging, and equally well suited to sailing in shallow waters, or beaching for loading cargo or undertaking basic repairs. Aboard, there was a hierarchy of officers and crew with specialist skills, and professionals trained through a sea-going 'apprenticeship'. Navigation required the quadrant and sextant for precise determination of latitude, while logs of astronomical observations, and later chronometers, helped determine longitude. An array of ancillary instruments was required for navigation and chart-making to address this critical problem of position at sea. Charts were essential for recording positions, and Cook retained a direct interest in their preparation, as he did in the constant recording of observations and comparing of calculations with predictions.

William Woollett (engraver, 1735–1785)
after William Hodges (1744–1797)
The Fleet of Otaheite Assembled at Oparee
London: Wm Strahan and Thos Cadell, 1777
Rex Nan Kivell Collection (Pictures), National Library
of Australia, Canberra, PIC Volume 566 #81654

Voyage artists depicted a variety of boats, from small bark canoes
to large Polynesian ocean-going vessels. Adapted to long-distance
voyaging, double-hulled canoes with sails and rig could track well
while sailing across the wind or reaching into the wind, with the
navigator 'reading' sailing directions or bearings to distant islands.
And, as Tupaia's map showed, this was a navigation system that
could be applied to other island groups, centred on his home island
of Ra'iatea.

FOLLOWING PAGES

William Faden (engraver, 1749-1836)
after Tupaia (surveyor, c. 1725–1770)
*A Chart Representing the Isles of the South Sea, According to the
Notions of the Inhabitants of O–Taheitee and the Neighbouring Isles,
Chiefly Collected from the Accounts of Tupaya*, in Johann Reinhold
Forster (1729–1798), *Observations Made during a Voyage Round
the World*
London: Printed for G. Robinson, 1778
Ferguson Collection (Australian Printed), National Library
of Australia, Canberra, FERG/7241

In his journal entry for 31 March 1770, Cook described Tupaia's
geographical knowledge as 'pretty extensive', listing the islands that
he and others had told the Europeans about: 'He at one time gave us
an Account of near 130 Islands but in his Chart he laid down only
74 and this is about the Number that some others of the Natives of
Otaheite gave us an account of.'

Printed by W. Hodges. Engraved by W. Woollett.

The Fleet of OTAHEITE *assembled at* OPÁREE.
Published Feb.¹ 1.ˢᵗ 1777, by W.ᵐ Strahan, New Street, Shoe Lane, & Tho.ˢ Cadell, in the Strand, London.

A CHART
representing the
ISLES of the SOUTH-SEA,
according to
the NOTIONS of the INHABITANTS of
o-TAHEITEE
and the Neighbouring Isles, chiefly
collected from the accounts of
TUPAYA.

I. of Danger or S. Bernardo

o-Ahourou 55

o-Rai-havai 53

o-Rima-tarra 52

o-Toomoo-papa 56

o-Raro-toa 54

o-Adeeha 49

Ururutu 48

o-Ahoua-hou 50

Touteepa 57

Navigators I.

o-Weeha 51

Woureeo 47

o-Reeva-vai 58

Mopeeha 44

Whennua-oora 45

o-Papatea 46

Tubs

21 Mouroa

Tainuna 59

o-Rotooma 61

Scilly I.

How's I.

19 Bow-bora

Tereati / Tootera } (West)

o-Poppoa 62

9 Raie

13 Ta
5.r Char

Palmerstones I.
o-Rimatema 60

Herveys I.
Moenotayo 63

o-Hitte-potto 65
Savage I.d

64 Te-Toopa-tupa-eahou

Oheavai 78

o-Hitte-toutou-atu 66

o-Hitte-toutou-nee 67

Te-Errepoo-opo-matte-hea 77

o-Hitte-toutou-rera 68

Ooporroo 76

Wouwou 75

Te-Orooro-Mativatea 74

o-Tootoo-erre 73

o-Hitte-taiterre 69

Te-Amaroo-hitte 70

Ouowhea 72

Te-Atou-hitte 71

Hoods I.

Dominica

42 o Heeva-roa   Teebooai 38

o Heeva-potto 43   Waitahoo or Whattarre-oora 39   o Nateya S.Pedro

S.Christina   Whattarretoah 36

Magdalena

o-Otto 41   Terowha 37

Te Manno 40

Neeo-heeva 35   o Haneanea 34

eiva 23   Georges I.   o Rima-roa 32

Waterland I   Oura 25   Teoheow 26   I. of Disappointment

Wahei 24

o-Anna 22   Pallisers I.

or Wales's I.   Patai 29   Carlshof   o-Heeva-toutou ai 33

rnicious I.   o Rairoa 27

Adventure I.d   Furneaux I.   Parallel of 17.° South Latit: Tatahaieta ⎫(East)

roa 9   o-Tah 28   o-Whateya 30   Ohe Tootera ⎭

HEITEE 1   o-Heeva-nooe 3   o-Whao 31   Doubtfull I   Resolution I

Mæatea 2   Chain I   Bird I

O snabrugh   Two Groups   Thrum Cap

Bow I.d   Lagoon I

4 Oirotah   Pr. Henry's I.d   Gloucester I.   Charlotte I.

Cumberland I   Egmont I.   Whitsunday I.

aio   Toometoa-roaro 3

Gloucester I.

Hitte-tamaroo-eiree 6

O snabrug Island

ito-nooe 11

Moutou 9

Tenew-hamea-tane 7   Onropoe 5

Pitcairn I.d

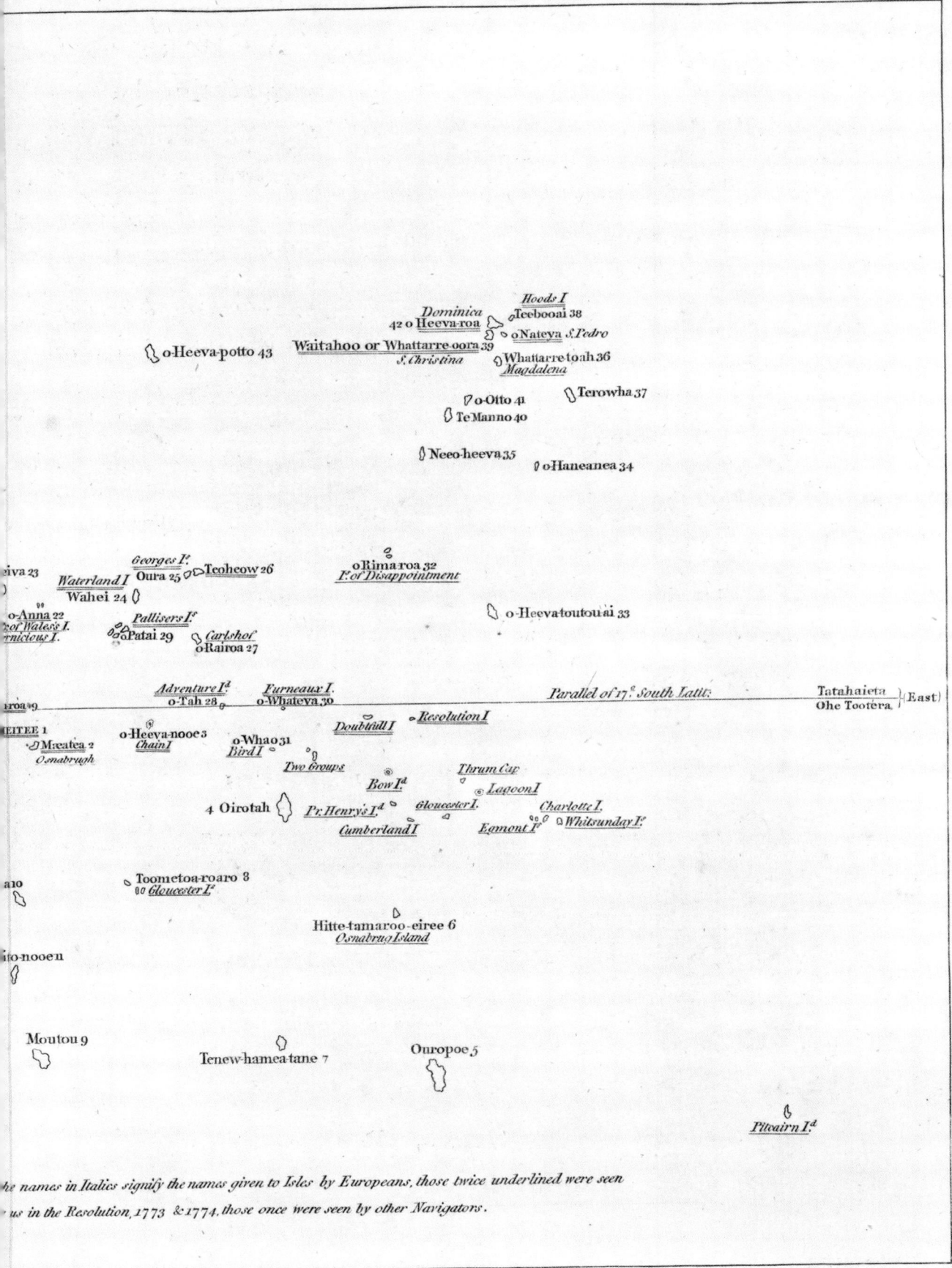

he names in Italics signify the names given to Isles by Europeans, those twice underlined were seen

us in the Resolution, 1773 & 1774, those once were seen by other Navigators.

W.m Faden sculp.

Drawn. from Nature by W.Hodges   Engraved by W.Watts

BOATS OF THE FRIENDLY ISLES.

Sandwich Sound.

Sandwich Sound.

P. W. Henry's Sound Capt.

John Webber (1752–1793)
People of Prince William Sound in Their Canoes 1778
in *A Voyage Round the World: But More Particularly to
the North-west Coast of America, Performed in 1785, 1786,
1787 and 1788, in the King George and Queen Charlotte,
Captains Portlock and Dixon*
London: George Goulding, 1789
Rex Nan Kivell Collection (Pictures), National Library of
Australia, Canberra, PIC Volume 42 #T2949 NK7402

The *Resolution* and *Discovery* spent just over a week in Prince
William Sound, Alaska, in May 1778. This study by voyage artist
John Webber details the canoes the local people used. In his journal,
Cook gives an evocative account of the encounter:

> They would not venture along side but kept talking to us at a distance,
> not one word of which we understood; they were cloathed in skins
> made into a dress like a shirt, or rather more like a wagonners frock,
> it reached nearly as low as the knee and their was no slit either behind
> or before. The Canoes were not built of wood like those of King Georges
> Sound; the frame only was of wood or slender laths and the out side
> sealskin, or the skin of some suchlike animal. When these people first
> came to the Ships, they displayed a white dress and unfolded their arms
> to the utmost extent, this we understood to be a sign of friendship and
> answered them in the same manner.

3819a
Endeavour
Box ☐ 66

Quarter Deck

Main Deck

Fore Castle

Companion

Main Hatch

Fore Hatch

Great Cabin

Captains Bedplace

Draughtsmen Cabins

Draughtsmen and Astronomers Bed Place

Pantry

After Hatch

Mr Banks Bedplace

Mr Greens Cabin

Draughtsmen Cabin

Pantry

Foremast Fall

Plans of His Majestys Bark
Endeavour, as fitted at Deptford,
in July 1768. —

Lower Deck

Sail Room

Boats Cabin

Boatswains Store Room

2d Lieutenant

Surgeon

Gunner

After Hatch

Main Hatch

Fore Hatch

Sail Room

Master

3d Lieut

Capt Cd

Carpenters Cabin

Carpenters Store Room

Well

Captains Store Room

Apr 1768
This Draught was sent to Deptford
fitt her for the South Sea
Returned the 18 Do

3814
Endeavour
Box ☐ 66

Ship Plans of HMB Endeavour 1768
© National Maritime Museum, Greenwich, London,
ZAZ6593 and ZAZ7844

These plans show how the former collier *Earl of Pembroke*, now
HMB *Endeavour*, was set up to serve as a suitable exploration vessel
for Cook's first Pacific voyage; they include the various deck layouts.
Originally built by Fishburn of Whitby, the ship was purchased
for £2,840 10s 11d. The alterations cost nearly twice as much.
Endeavour was classified as a 'bark' or bluff-bowed boat of shallow
draught. If grounded in shallow water, as was the case at Endeavour
Reef, it had a much better chance of floating off than did typical
vessels of the Royal Navy.

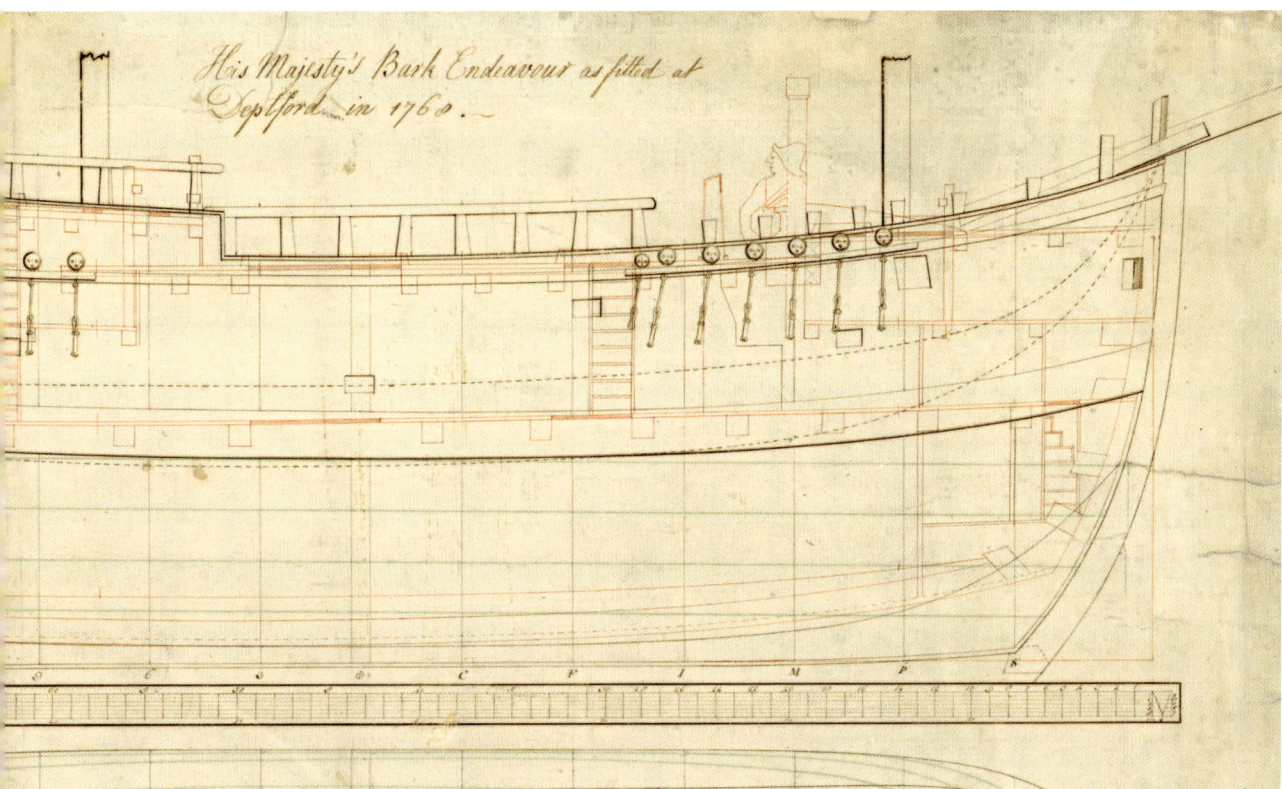

Cannon from HMB Endeavour, Which Was Jettisoned on the Great Barrier Reef in 1770 and Recovered in 1969 (with Replica Wheelhouse) 1725–50
National Museum of Australia, Canberra, 1981.0009.0001
Photo George Serras, National Museum of Australia

The 1969 archaeological expedition at Endeavour Reef, North Queensland, yielded a rich range of objects from the *Endeavour*: cannon and cannon balls, 'kentledge' (permanent iron ballast) and stone ballast from New Zealand. Having spent centuries beneath the waves, the cannon had become encrusted with coral.

Coral Concretion from One of the Cannon of HMB Endeavour with the Cipher of King George II before 1969
Australian National Maritime Museum, Sydney, 00029235

James Cook (1728–1779)
Letter to Captain William Hammond from the Resolution at Madeira 1 August 1772
Captain Cook Memorial Museum, Whitby, WHICC.185.1
© CCMM Whitby

In this letter Cook reports on how the *Resolution* and *Adventure* had performed on the journey from Plymouth to Madeira. They were converted colliers, built in Whitby, and had been purchased from Captain William Hammond for use on Cook's second Pacific voyage.

> *I had opportunities to try the Resolution and Adventure and have the pleasure to acqt you that I find them answer in all respects as well as I could wish: the Resolution so far from being Crank is remarkably Stiff, her Enemies must now be silent on that head—In point of Sailing they are very well matched there is however some advantage in favour of the Resolution, upon the whole I think they both sail very well.*

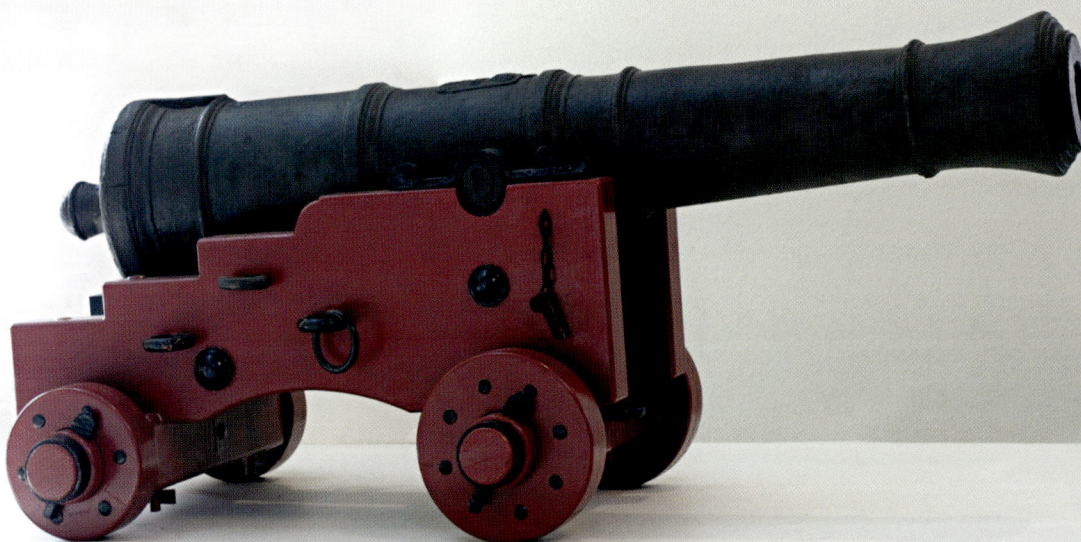

Dear Sir   Resolution at Madeira 1st: Augst: 72

      Three days ago I arrived at this place
after a Passage of Sixteen days from Plymouth
in which I had oppertunities to try the Resolution
and Adventure and have the pleasure to acqt:
you that I find them answer in all respects
as well as I could wish, the Resolution so far
from being Crank is remarkably Stiff her
Enemies must now be silent on that head ——
      In point of Sailing they are very well matched
there is however some advantage in favour
of the Resolution, upon the whole I think they
both sail very well and as a further satisfaction
I have got a set of very good Men who seem
happy in their respective Situations ———
      I beg you will make my respectfull Compliments
to Sr George Saville and if you should happen
to go to Whitby remember me to my good
friend Captain Walker. I intend to put
to Sea this Evening and shall hardly stop any
Where till I get to the Cape from which place
you will probalby hear again from him who is
With great truth and Sincerity
        D Sir
         your much obliged Humble Servt:
             Jams Cook

Contemporary Plan of the Resolution c. 1772
Mulgrave Archives, Lent by the Marquis of Normanby,
WHICC.139

For Cook's second Pacific voyage, the *Resolution* was originally
modified to accommodate the requirements of Joseph Banks
and his party. On a trial run, however, the changes were found
to have made the ship top heavy, and therefore unseaworthy.
This is the only existing plan showing the changes.

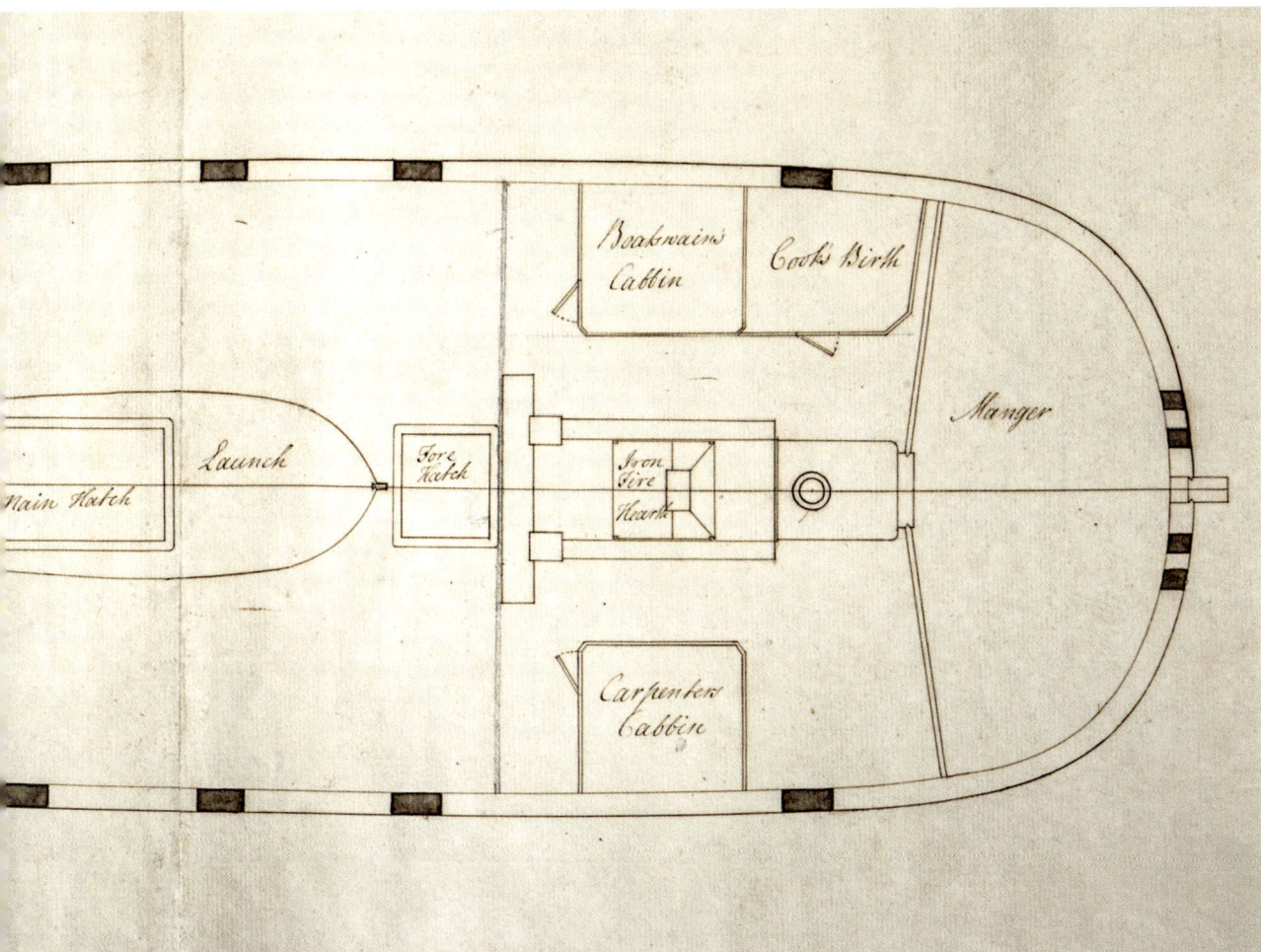

Boatswain's Cabbin

Cook's Birth

Manger

Main Hatch

Launch

Fore Hatch

Iron Fire Hearth

Carpenters Cabbin

TOP

Plane Table Frame Used by Captain James Cook 1768–79
National Museum of Australia, Canberra, 2006.0089.0001
Photo Lannon Harley, National Museum of Australia

The frame held drawing paper firmly onto a board or plane table. Maps were drawn with reference to graduated degree scales on the face of the frame.

BOTTOM

Captain Cook's Scale of Sines for Navigation Purposes 1770
State Library of New South Wales, Sydney, SAFE/DR 12

The sector, or proportional compass, was an instrument used for mathematical calculations, such as taking square and cube roots. This sector is believed to have been among those instruments Cook gave to the British naval scholar Dr William Burney.

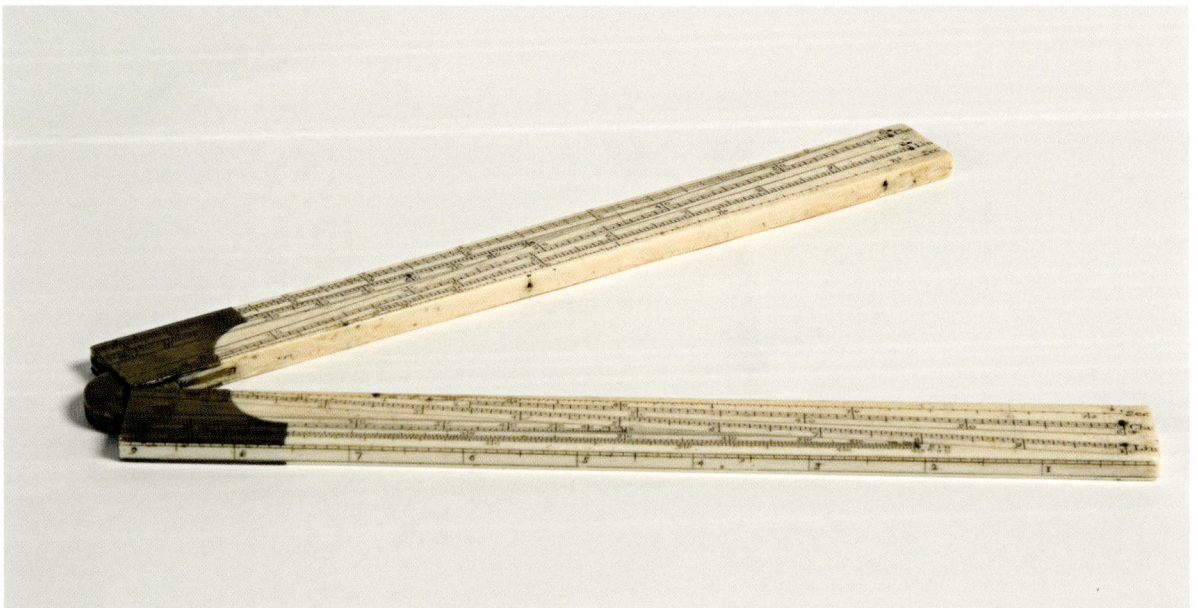

Nevil Maskelyne (1732–1811)
The Nautical Almanac and Astronomical Ephemeris,
for the Year 1769
London: W. Richardson and S. Clark, 1768
Maps Collection, National Library of Australia, Canberra,
MAP Ra 379

The *Nautical Almanac* was a record of the positions of celestial bodies for the purpose of enabling navigators to determine the position of their ships while at sea. In celestial navigation, lunar distance (the angular distance between the moon and another celestial body) is used to calculate Greenwich time. By comparing Greenwich to the local time, the navigator could determine longitude.

[60]   M A Y 1769.

Configurations of the SATELLITES of JUPITER
at 9 o' th' Clock in the Evening.

J U N E 1769.   [61]

Days of the Month.	Days of the Week.	Sundays, Holidays, &c.	Phases of the Moon.
			D h '
			New Moon — 3. 20. 22
			First Quarter — 10. 17. 1
1	Th.	Nicomede.	Full Moon — 18. 20. 15
2	F.		Last Quarter — 26. 12. 46
3	Sa.	K. Geo. III. born.	
4	Su.	2d Sunday after Trinity.	
5	M.	Boniface. In 15 days	Other Phenomena.
6	Tu.	[of H. Trin. 3 ret. D.	
7	W.		3. ☉ eclipsed, visible.
8	Th.		♀ passes over ☉.
9	F.		h ʹ
10	Sa.	Pri. Amelia born.	Beg. of Ing. cent. ☉ 7. 13
11	Su.	3d. Su. after Tr. St. Barn.	Total Ingress — 7. 32
12	M.	In 3 weeks of H. Tr. 4 ret.	Beg. of Egress — 13. 14
13	Tu.		Total Egress — 13. 33
14	W.	Term ends.	Beg. of Ingress at
15	Th.		Greenwich — 7. 6
16	F.		Total Ingress — 7. 25
17	Sa.	S. Alban.	4. ☾ infra cornu bor. ♉
18	Su.	4th Sunday after Trinity.	12h. 53ʹ.
19	M.		☾ ♨ Ⅱ 22h. 22ʹ.
20	Tu.	Transf. of Edw. K. of	5. ☾ μ Ⅱ 1h. 21ʹ.
21	W.	[W. Sax.	☾ ζ Ⅱ 17h. 0ʹ.
22	Th.		7. ♀ ☉ Ⅱ diff. Lat. 3ʹ.
23	F.		8. ☾ ξ ♌ 6h. 47ʹ.
24	Sa.	Nativity of St. John Bapt.	☾ ο ♌ 12h. 49ʹ.
25	Su.	5th Sunday after Trinity.	☾ π ♌ 22h. 6ʹ.
26	M.		10. ☾ ε ♌ 18h. 25ʹ.
27	Tu.		16. ☾ ♌ ♍ 9h. 52ʹ.
28	W.		18. ☾ θ Ophiuchi 0h. 4ʹ.
29	Th.	St. Peter.	☾ B Ophiuchi 1h. 57ʹ.
30	F.		☽ eclipsed invisible.
			19. ☾ ο ♐ 23h. 25ʹ.
			20. ☾ π ♐ 1h. 55ʹ.
			☉ enters ♋ at 17h.
			56ʹ.
			24. ♀ ε ♉ diff. Lat. 1°. 5ʹ.
			25. ♀ Stationary.
			27. ☾ ♨ ♓ 19h. 58ʹ.

43

John Arnold (1736–1799)
Marine Chronometers Used on Cook's Second Pacific Voyage 1771
Royal Society, London, Ref No. T/002 and Ref No. T/003

These brass chronometers are two of three by John Arnold that were taken on the voyage. Arnold was a London watch- and clock-maker who had begun to experiment with the making of marine timekeepers in the late 1760s. Following negotiations with the Board of Longitude, it was agreed to test them against Larcum Kendall's copy of John Harrison's fourth marine timekeeper ('K1') on the *Resolution* and the *Adventure*. On the voyage, 'K1' performed 'magnificently', while the Arnold proved erratic. Although his timepieces did not perform well in this trial, Arnold's later chronometers included newly designed components and were used by the British Admiralty and the East India Company.

Cook's Holograph Journal, Second Pacific Voyage (detail)
28 November 1771 – 10 November 1774
British Library, London, Add MS 27886, f.30r
© British Library Board

In his journal entries for Saturday 30 October 1772, Cook records:

Messrs Wales and Baily, the two astronomers were on shore all the time making the necessary astronomical observations in order to ascertain the going of the Watches and other purposes: Mr Kendall's Watch thus far has been found to answer beyond all expect[at]ion, but this cannot be said of Mr Arnolds … however one of Mr Arnolds on board the Adventure kept time in such a Manner as not be complained on.

FOLLOWING PAGE

*Certificate Recommending the Election of James Cook
as a Fellow of the Royal Society 1775–76*
Royal Society, London, EC/1775/27

Cook's scientific achievements were recognised by his being admitted as a Fellow of the Royal Society on 7 March 1776. His certificate was endorsed by a greater number of fellows than was usually the case, including many prominent ones such as Joseph Banks and Nevil Maskelyne, suggesting that the Society's support for Cook was strong. It reads:

Captain James Cook, of Mile-end a gentleman skilfull in astronomy, & the succesful conductor of two important voyages for the discovery of unknown countries, by which geography & natural history have been greatly advantaged & improved, being desirous of the honour of becoming a member of this Society, we whose names are underwritten, do, from our personal knowledge testify, that we believe him deserving of such honour, and that he will become a worthy & useful member.

Mr Kendalls Watch, thus far has been found to answer beyond all expection, but this cannot be said of Mr Arnolds. The Longitude of the Cape Town pointed out by these Watches is already mentioned in their proper columns. by observation made here, Mr Kendals Watch is found to have altered its rate of going something more than one second pr Day, by going 7/8 of a second pr Day on mean time whereas at Greenwich it lost 6/8 pr Day, this variation however is very inconsiderable. Mr Arnolds was found to loose on Mean time, by the mean rate of its going for twelve days 1..31,0125 per day which is 1..17,63 more than at Greenwich, and also varied in its rate sometimes more than half a minute pr Day. however one of Mr Arnolds on board the Adventure kept time in such a manner as not to be complained on ——

Mr Forster met with a Swedish Gentleman here, one Mr Sparman, who understood something of Botany and Natural History and who was willing to embarque with us. Mr Forster thinking that he would be of great assistance to him in the course of the Voyage strongly importuned me to take him on board which I accordingly did——

Mr Shank first Lieutenant of the Adventure having been in an ill state of health ever since we left England and not recovering here, requested my leave to quit in order to return home for the reestablishment of his health; his request appearing to be will founded I gave him leave accordingly and appointed Mr Burney one of my Midshipmen Second Lieutenant of the Adventure in the room of Mr Kemp whom I appointed first—

of Mile-end

Captain James Cook, a gentleman skilfull in astronomy, & the successful conductor of two important voyages for the discovery of unknown countries, by which geography & natural history have been greatly advantaged & improved, being desirous of the honour of becoming a member of this Society, we whose names are underwritten, do, from our personal knowledge testify, that we believe him deserving of such honour, and that he will become a worthy & useful member.

Nov. 23. 1775   Jos: Banks.

Decr 7. 1775   Dan. Solander

—14   Mulgrave   John Reinold Forster.

Jany 11. 1776   Seaforth

—18   Blagden.

—25   C. Morton

—1

—8   H. Cavendish

—15   J. Cuthbert

—22

Ballotted Feb 29. 1776
Signed Bond
Do Mar. 7. 1776   John Hunter

James Burrow.

J Boyd

N. Maskelyne

Matt Raper.

S. Horsley

Jnº Campbell

James Stuart

Daniel Wray

Ph. Stephens

Jnº Ibbetson

Alexr Aubert

Robert Mylne

Edward Poore.

Mat. Duane.

Antº Shepherd

3. TOTAIETE MÄ

Over the three Pacific voyages, Totaiete mä (Society Islands) held a special place for Cook and his men. They found these islands—especially Tahiti, Moorea, Huahine, Ra'iatea and Bora Bora, now part of French Polynesia—to be a kind of Arcadia at times. Relationships with Society Islanders evolved, beginning in Tahiti, which was recommended by Samuel Wallis, commander of the *Dolphin* voyage (1766–68), as being ideal for observing the 1769 transit of Venus.

Indeed, the main aim of Cook's *Endeavour* voyage (1768–71) was to observe this transit from southern skies. By the early eighteenth century, recording the transit of visible planets across the face of the sun was seen as having great scientific importance, part of the quest to find a reliable way of determining longitude. In 1716 Edmond Halley showed how these transits could be used, through observations made from different points scattered around the globe, to calculate the mean distance between the Earth and Venus and, consequently, the mean distance between the Earth and the Sun (the 'astronomical unit'). From this, the scale of the whole solar system could be determined. Halley urged the scientific community to apply this technique to the upcoming transits (1761 and 1769). Observations of the 1761 transit were uncoordinated, so great efforts were made by the scientific bodies of Europe to do better next time. The Royal Society sponsored five expeditions, of which the *Endeavour* voyage was one. Cook and his fellow astronomer Charles Green made observations from Tahiti at a location still known as Point Venus.

Between 1769 and Cook's last visit in 1777, interactions with Society Islanders were extensive. Europeans and islanders explored many aspects of personal, social and cultural exchange. Knowledge was shared, relationships formed and broken, and trade in sex, goods and tattoos flourished, sometimes in a spirit of civility. At times Cook sought to apply British concepts of property and justice, while also observing local custom, or joining in performances (*heiva*) and rituals. Both the British and the islanders were changed, and both advanced their own causes.

Samuel Middiman (engraver, 1750–1831)
after Sydney Parkinson (artist, c. 1745–1771)
Venus Fort, Erected by the Endeavour's People, to Secure
Themselves during the Observation of the Transit of Venus,
at Otaheite
London: Stanfield Parkinson, 1773
Rex Nan Kivell Collection (Pictures), National Library
of Australia, Canberra, PIC Drawer 7434 #U3047 NK2140/A

William Hodges (1744–1797)
View from Point Venus, Island of Otaheite c. 1774
Pictures Collection, National Library of Australia, Canberra,
PIC Screen 58 #R8849

William Hodges was appointed draughtsman in Johann Zoffany's
place after the withdrawal of Joseph Banks and his retinue from
Cook's second Pacific voyage. Hodges specialised in landscapes,
and duly delivered a series of spectacular oil paintings to the
Admiralty in the years after the voyage. His work deftly captured
the light of lands hitherto unseen by European artists, in a way
that owes more to the seventeenth-century artist Claude Lorrain
than to nascent Romanticism.

James Cook (1728–1779)
Observations and Remarks on the Transit of Venus 3 June 1769
State Library of New South Wales, Sydney, SAFE 1/66

Great care was taken by the men of the *Endeavour* to prepare
for the transit of Venus. Arriving with weeks to spare, they built
a fort at Point Venus, and observations were recorded, eventually
to be published in *Philosophical Transactions*, the journal of the
Royal Society. Cook and astronomer Charles Green made further
observations, until their makeshift observatory was dismantled on
8 July.

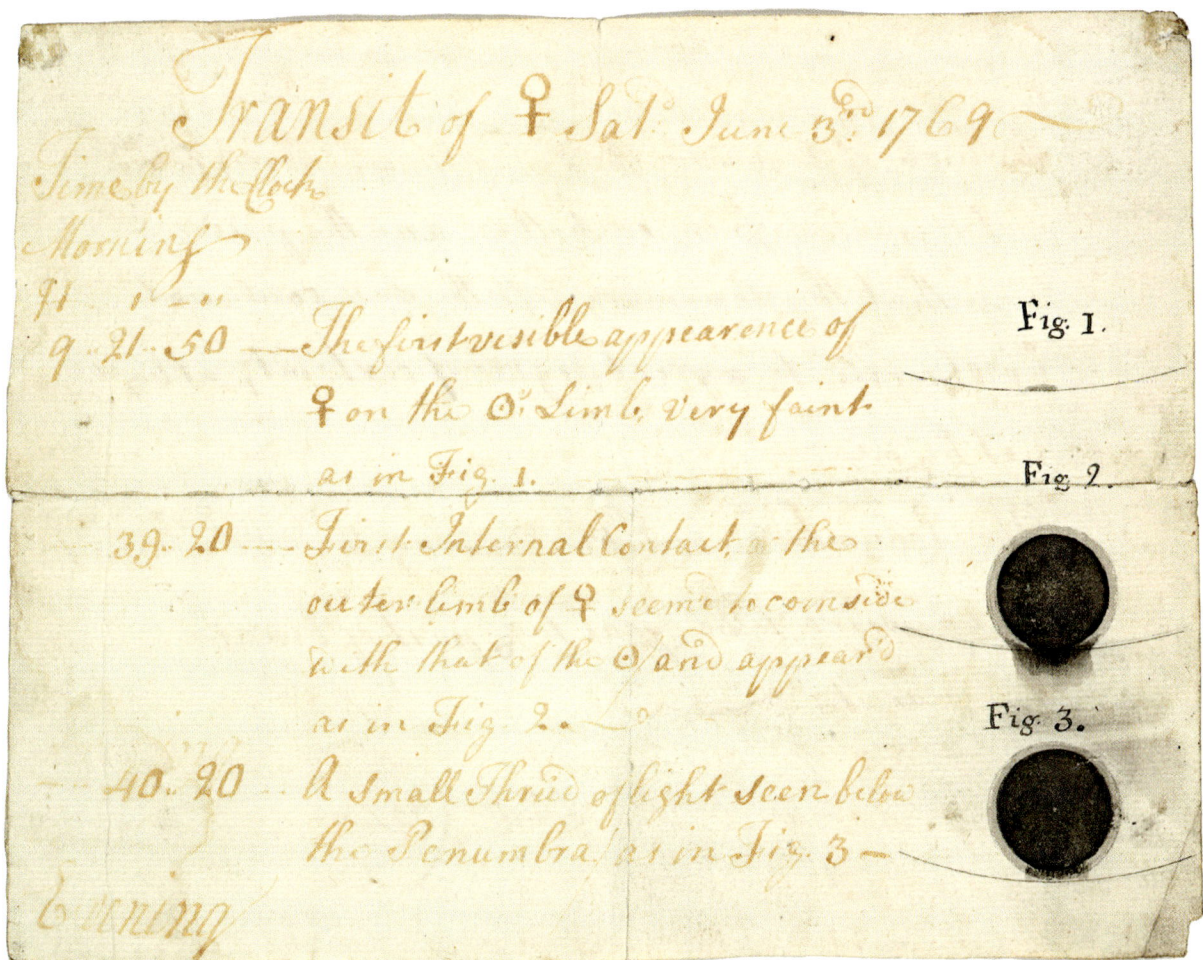

William Hodges (1744–1797)
Portrait of Tynai-mai, Princess of Raiatea c. 1773
Pictures Collection, National Library of Australia, Canberra,
PIC Drawer 8 #R739

Hodges also produced a series of developed chalk drawings, with a
view to their being engraved to illustrate the official voyage account.
The National Library of Australia holds 18. Six are of people of
the Society Islands, including Tynai-mai of Ra'iatea. In his account
of the voyage, naturalist Georg Forster (son of Johann Reinhold
Forster) gave this description of her: 'Her eyes were full of fire and
expression, and an agreeable smile sat in her round face. Mr. Hodges
took this opportunity of drawing a sketch of her portrait, which her
vivacity and restless disposition rendered almost impossible.'

OPPOSITE

William Hodges (1744–1797)
Otoo, King of Otaheite 1773
Pictures Collection, National Library of Australia, Canberra,
PIC Drawer 12 #R755

The British Pacific voyages of the 1760s and 1770s coincided with
a revolution in Tahiti, and later one man, Tu, rose to become king
of all its peoples. Tu, who was called Otoo by the Europeans, went
on to found, in 1788, a dynasty under the name Pōmare I. He
is depicted here in one of Hodges' finest portraits. Georg Forster
described him thus: 'His head, notwithstanding a certain gloominess
which seemed to express a fearful disposition, had a majestic and
intelligent air, and there was great expression in his full black eyes.'

James Cook (1728–1779) and Isaac Smith (1752–1831)
*A Plan of King Georges Island or Otaheite Lying in the
South Sea* 1769
State Library of New South Wales, Sydney, SAFE/DLSPENCER 168

Cook's journal entry for 26 June 1769 records that he 'set out in the
Pinnace' with Banks and 'one of ye Natives with an intent to make
the Circuit of the Island in order to examine and draw a Sketch of
the Coast and Harbours thereof'. It took him a number of days to
complete this map (one of several versions he made): 'The Plan or
Sketch which I have drawn, altho it cannot be very accurate yet it
will be found sufficient to point out the Situations of the different
Bays and harbours and the figure of the Island and I believe is
without any material error.'

**'Cook is very renowned amongst Polynesians to have been an
excellent navigator and good observer. This map shows the
several valleys, villages and rivers of Tahiti.'**

**Natea Montillier Tetuanui, Tahiti, Cultural office of
French Polynesia**

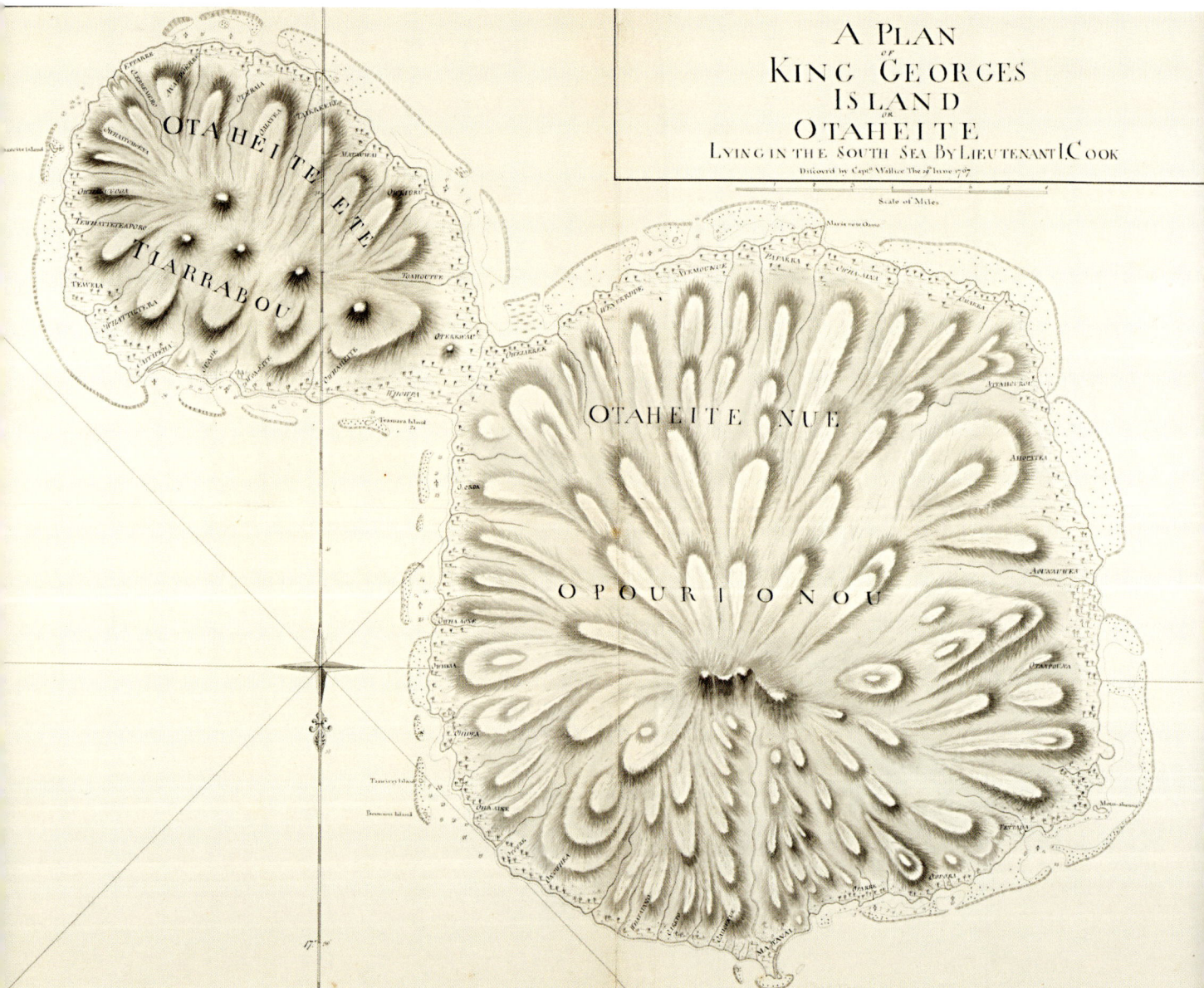

Tāumi (Breast Ornament) 1760s or 1770s
Australian Museum, Sydney, H000145

Tāumi were traditionally worn in Tahitian society to protect or decorate the chest and signify status. They were collected on all Cook's voyages, and this example is believed to have been in Cook's own collection.

'Today dance groups, chiefs and orators still wear this *tāumi* (breast ornament) made of weaving or wood, decorated with tapa, tied feathers and mother of pearl, shell or teeth. Dog's hair and human teeth are no longer used.'

Natea Montillier Tetuanui, Tahiti, Cultural office of French Polynesia

Attributed to Sydney Parkinson (c. 1745–1771)
Bread Fruit 1769
Rex Nan Kivell Collection (Pictures), National Library
of Australia, Canberra, PIC Drawer 3466 #T2501 NK1223

The dispersal of *Artocarpus altilis* (breadfruit) across the Pacific
was dependent on human seafaring. Banks and others saw the
value of this high-yielding food plant, and it was introduced as
a high-energy food source in British colonies in the Caribbean.

OPPOSITE

John Webber (1752–1793)
A Portrait of Poedua c. 1782
Rex Nan Kivell Collection (Pictures), National Library
of Australia and National Gallery of Australia, Canberra,
PIC T520 NK 5192

Poetua (Poedua) was a princess of Ra'iatea, the daughter of Orio.
Cook first met her on his second Pacific voyage, and she was known
for her graceful dancing. Here she is older, and pregnant, as she was
when Cook visited again in late 1777. Cook anchored at Ra'iatea
in November and December. On 24 November, two crew members
deserted from *Discovery*. To ensure their return, Poetua, her
brother and her husband were all held captive. It was under these
circumstances that Poetua posed for Webber aboard the *Discovery*.

Webber's portrait is one of the earliest images of a Polynesian
woman Europeans would have seen. Three versions of the
painting survive.

'She is wrapped with *pāreu* (cloth) made of white tapa going
down to the knees, which women of all ranks used to make.
White tapa is made with 'uru (breadfruit) bark. The refinement
and white colour of the tapa, the *tāhiri* (fan) made of wood, the
nape (string of coconut husk fibres) and frizzy hair, as well as her
posture show us that she belongs to the chief family. Her released
brown undulating hair down on her shoulders and fair skin are
also signs of her aristocratic status as lower caste women had
shorter hair. Nudity above the navel is often a pride for young
ladies, but they could also tie the *pāreu* on one shoulder.'

**Natea Montillier Tetuanui, Tahiti, Cultural office of
French Polynesia**

Bread Fruit

Unknown artist
after John Frederick Miller (1759–1796)
Tools from the Society Islands 1773
Kerry Stokes Collection, Perth, 2012.070.02

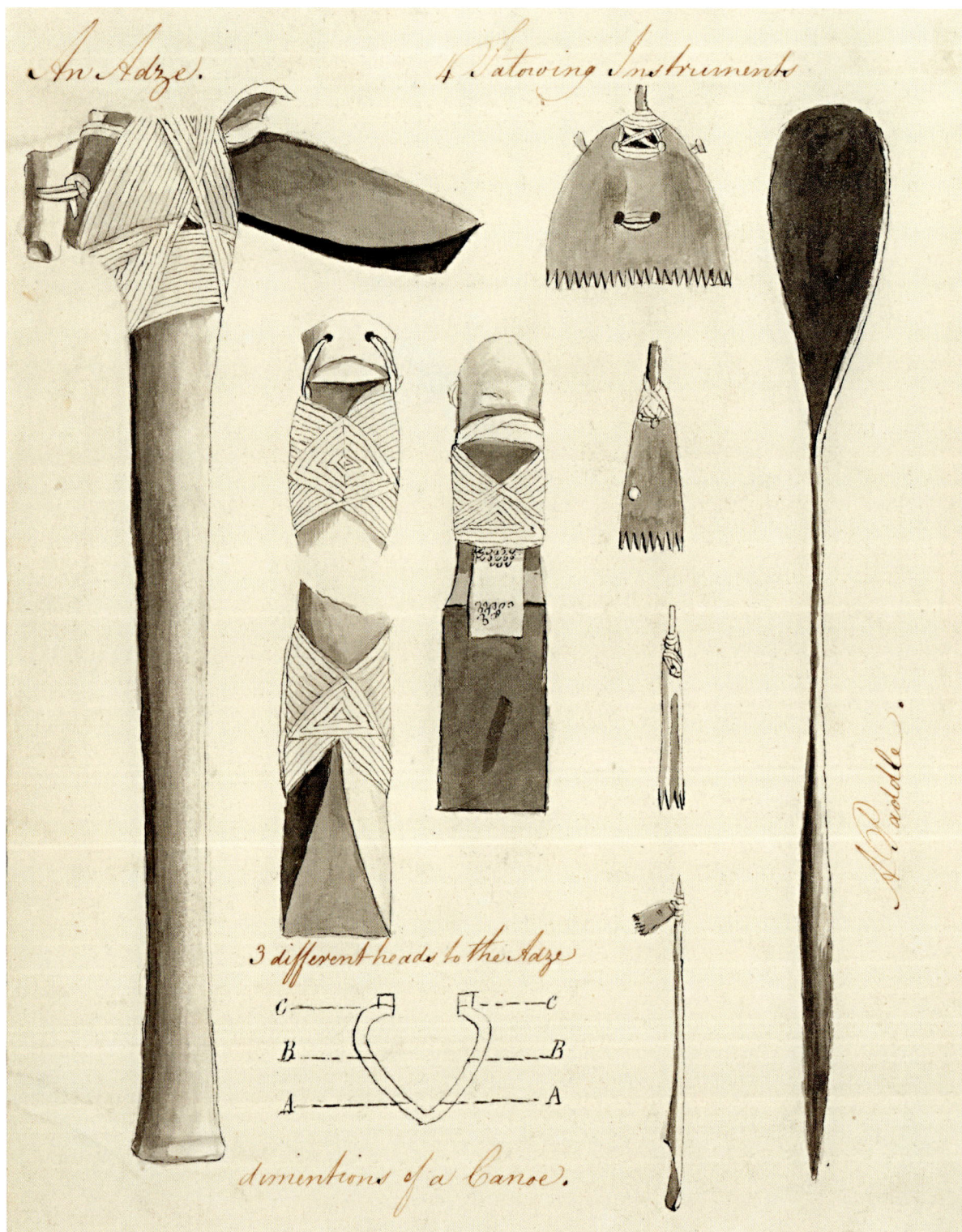

An Adze.

4 Tatowing Instruments

3 different heads to the Adze

C ———— C
B ———— B
A ———— A

dimentions of a Canoe.

A Paddle.

Tahitian Tattooing Mallet 1700s
Collection of the Museum of New Zealand
Te Papa Tongarewa, FE003009
Gift of the Imperial Institute, 1955

'Tattoos in Polynesia covered the body (face, neck, chest,
armpits, arms, hands, legs, feet, anus) and even the late chief's
skull, most often from the hips to the knees, making the person
look as if he wore clothes, with patterns which would trace the
memory of events (death, birth of a child, the social position,
the passage of puberty), natural elements (flora, fauna),
geometrical symbols representing a clan, a god, a totem animal
which have similarities with the Pascuan *rogorogo* ideograms.
They would vary according to the origins of the individual.
Tattoos were meant to exalt sexual attraction, inspire terror to
the enemies. They matched with the splendid ornaments worn
for celebrations. They were restricted for young women on the
body parts under the clothes, on the waist, the lips, the chin
(as an exception, only women used to be tattooed in Fiji). The
bloodshed is a proof of courage, a sacred ritual, linked to the
metaphysical. People believed they would bring the person a
magic power against diseases, recover wounds, help procreate
and give birth. The tattooing is close to another rite, the
scarification which was performed on the skull, on the tongue,
for a relative's or a chief's funerals.'

Natea Montillier Tetuanui, Tahiti, Cultural office of
French Polynesia

Ta (Tahitian Tattooing Implement) 1700s
Collection of the Museum of New Zealand
Te Papa Tongarewa, FE003010
Gift of the Imperial Institute, 1955

Unknown artist
after Sydney Parkinson (c. 1745–1771) and
after John James Barralet (c. 1747–1815)
A View in the Island of Otaheite with the House Called
Tupapow, Under Which the Dead are Deposited 1773
Kerry Stokes Collection, Perth, 2012.070.07

This is a copy of a copy of an original work by Sydney Parkinson, whose journal records on 5 May 1769: 'In walking through the woods we saw the corpse of a man laid out on a sort of bier, which had an awning over it of mats, supported by four sticks; a square piece of ground around it was railed in with bamboos, and the body was covered with cloth.'

'A *fare tūpapa'u* (house for embalming) was built for chiefs. The *tahu'a miri* (embalmer) would *tāmiri* (extract) organs from the guts and skull, fill them with scented plants like the *miri* (basilic and fragrant resins) there, anoint the skin with perfumed oil, let the corpse dry out of its flesh, mucus and blood on the *tu'ura'a-turuma* or *taha-tūpāpa'u* … which was placed on a platform higher than that of a house, near or on the marae, at more than ten feet from a house because of the smell. Then he would *ha'apa'a* (mummify) the body by wrapping it in perfumed tapa and a mat, often in a sitting position. The roof was meant to prevent rain from ruining the embalming process.'

Natea Montillier Tetuanui, Tahiti, Cultural office of
French Polynesia

OPPOSITE

'Chief Mourner's' Costume (partial)
from the Society Islands 1700s
Collection of the Museum of New Zealand
Te Papa Tongarewa, Wellington, FE000336/1–5
Gift of Lord St Oswald, 1912

In the funerary rituals that followed the death of a chief, the 'Chief Mourner' (usually a relative of the deceased) would rampage around the village, accompanied by a group of attendants, scaring all who crossed his path. On one occasion, on 10 June 1769, Joseph Banks was permitted to play the role of one of the attendants.

One of at least 10 collected on Cook's second Pacific voyage, this example is incomplete. They were highly valuable in the eighteenth century, as they were made of rare materials and required an expert craftsperson.

'The *tahu'a heva* (mourner priest) wore a *pū-tahi* (costume) during the *heva* (mourning ceremony) or *pūtopo-pau* reserved for *ari'i* (chiefs). People fled when the priest approached the village … as he makes his *tete* (mother of pearl castanettes) clink and as his warriors catch one or more victims designated by him for the human sacrifice to be held on the *marae* (sacred place).'

Natea Montillier Tetuanui, Tahiti, Cultural office of
French Polynesia

William Wade Ellis (1751–1785)
Inland View of Oitapeeah Bay in the Island Otaheite 1777
Rex Nan Kivell Collection (Pictures), National Library of
Australia, Canberra, PIC Solander Box B7 #T229 NK6577

Surgeon's mate William Ellis rendered this view inland from Tautira
on the south-eastern coast of Tahiti in August 1777. In his voyage
account, he wrote: 'The face of the country here exhibits a very
different appearance from that of the Friendly Isles. Mountains and
vallies, hills and dales, and in short every thing to conspire to form
the most romantic views imaginable.'

4. SOUTH PACIFIC

Cook's expeditions visited many South Pacific island groups, where they documented the people and their way of life. They collected botanical and zoological specimens and craft objects. Interactions between the Indigenous people and the Europeans were mixed. Things had begun disastrously, with the deaths of Maori people at Turanganui River in 1769. However, relations improved on later voyages, and the logs and journals of Cook and others contain extensive descriptions of both New Zealand and its people.

Trade, or the exchange of goods, gifts or favours, was an ever-present part of the relationship. In many places a brisk trade in iron nails developed, in exchange for tapa and other artefacts, food, labour or sex. Though Cook often made efforts to respect local customs, inevitably such exchanges were sometimes conducted without regard for social structures or taboo systems.

On his second and third voyages, Cook reached the islands of Tonga on three occasions. He called them the 'Friendly Islands', unaware of growing Tongan resentment and plans to drive off the Europeans. The skilful portraits executed by William Hodges, obtained during fleeting visits to Rapa Nui (Easter Island) and the Marquesas Islands, belied how little cultural exchange had actually been accomplished. In contrast to the sometimes friendly, if misunderstood, commerce between the outsiders and some Polynesian peoples, relations with the Melanesian peoples of New Caledonia and Vanuatu (New Hebrides) were brief, and landing parties often encountered massed groups of armed men.

Thomas Chambers (engraver, 1724–1789),
after Sydney Parkinson (artist, c. 1747–1771)
The Head of a Chief of New Zealand, the Face Curiously Tataowd,
or Marked, According to Their Manner 1773
Rex Nan Kivell Collection (Pictures), National Library
of Australia, Canberra, PIC Drawer 3584 #U2775 NK

By the time the *Endeavour* voyage reached New Zealand, Sydney
Parkinson gained a new confidence as an artist. This is one of two
famous Maori portraits Chambers produced, based on Parkinson's
originals, which were probably done of the men from Poverty Bay
who visited the ship on 12 October 1769. Parkinson wrote in his
journal: 'Most of them had their hair tied up on the crown of their
heads in a knot … Their faces were tataowed, or marked either all
over, or on one side, in a very curious manner, some of them in
fine spiral directions like a volute, being indented in the skin very
different from the rest'.

John Cleveley (c. 1745–1786)
Discovery and Resolution at an Island in the Pacific 1777
c. 1780s
Rex Nan Kivell Collection (Pictures), National Library
of Australia, Canberra, PIC Screen 106 #1349

Cleveley's painting was created to respond to the growing popular demand in England for images of the Pacific. It brings together depictions of different Pacific sailing vessels, set against an imagined backdrop of land and sea.

The artist never sailed with Cook, though he had been slated to go on the second Pacific voyage as part of Joseph Banks' retinue. Instead, he accompanied Banks to Iceland. The Cleveleys were a family of marine artists, and John's brother James was carpenter aboard the *Resolution* on Cook's third voyage. James is known to have drawn on the voyage, and likely shared his work with his brother upon his return to England.

James Cook (1728–1779) and Isaac Smith (1752–1831)
A Chart of Part of New Zeland, or the Island of Tovypoenammu
Lying in the South Sea 1770
State Library of New South Wales, Sydney, SAFE/DLSPENCER 166 B

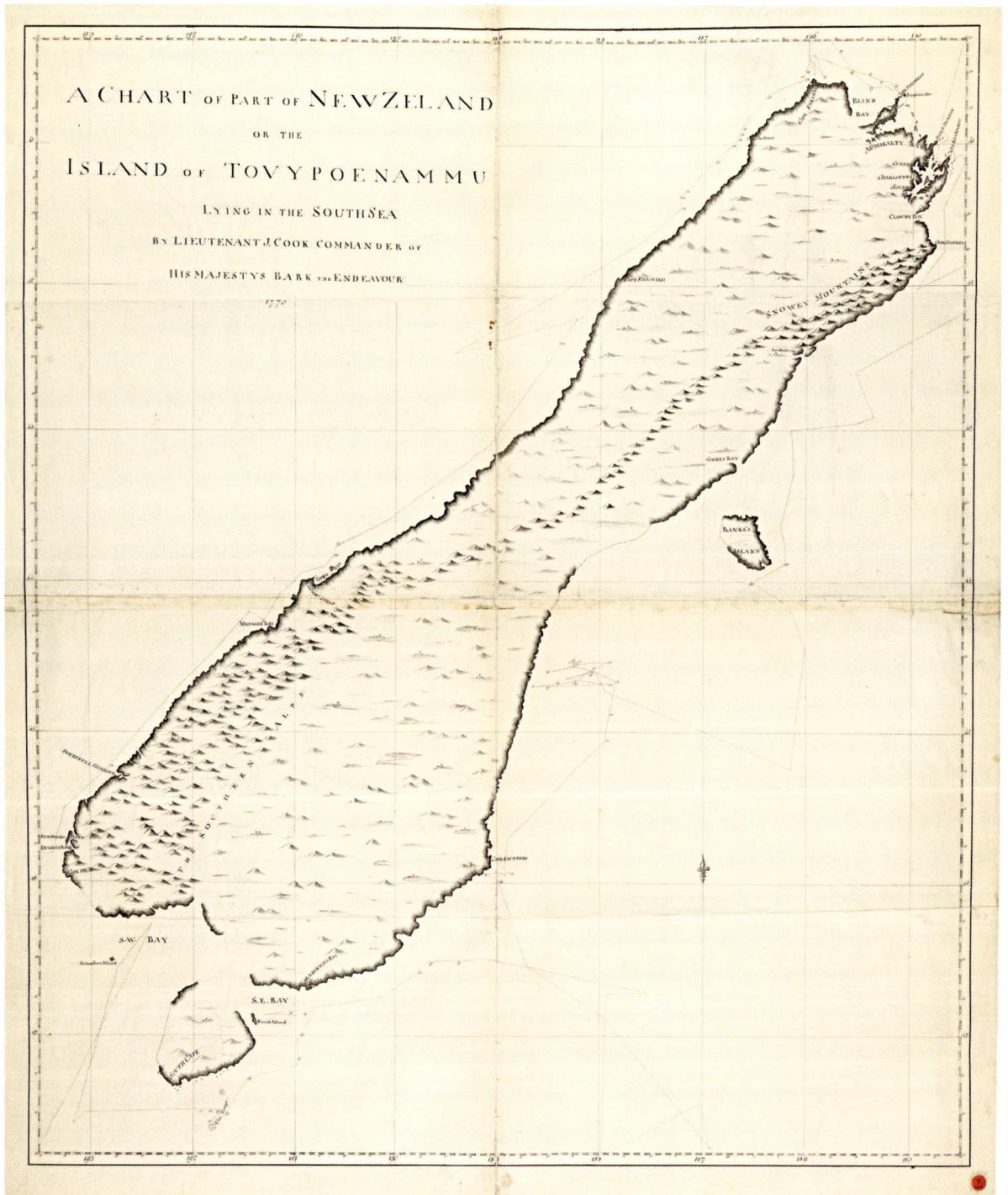

James Cook (1728–1779) and Isaac Smith (1752–1831)
A Chart of Part of New Zeland or the Island of Aeheinomowe Lying in the South Seas [North Island] 1770
State Library of New South Wales, Sydney, SAFE/DLSPENCER 166 A

This map and its companion for the South Island—constituting the first complete mapping of New Zealand—chart the journey of the *Endeavour* as it made its first recorded circumnavigation of that country. The most heavily named and closely surveyed area is the north-east coast of the North Island. The chart names mountains and ranges, such as Southern Alps, Mount Egmont, Mount Edgecumbe,

and several coastal areas, including Cape Kidnappers, Cape Palliser, Hawkes Bay, Bay of Islands, Bay of Plenty, Tolaga Bay, Poverty Bay, Queen Charlotte Sound.

A CHART OF PART OF NEW ZELAND OR THE ISLAND OF AEHEINOMOWE LYING IN THE SOUTH SEAS BY LIEUT. J. Cook. COMMANDER OF His Majesty's BARK the ENDEAVOUR. 1770

Richard Pickersgill (1749–1779)
*A Chart of the North East Coast of New Zealand
from Mercury Bay to Bay of Islands* 1769
The National Archives, UK, ADM 352/671
© Crown Copyright – image courtesy of The National Archives

Pickersgill, master's mate in *Endeavour*, was a Cook protégé, and this
hand-drawn chart is one of a number of detailed charts and plans
he produced during the voyage. Oriented with south at the top, it
shows the north-east coast of New Zealand, from the mouth of the
'River Thames' (Waihou River) to the Bay of Islands.

Cook wrote in his journal (5 December 1769) about the abundance
of fish in the Bay of Islands, which he named 'on account of the
great number which line its shores and these help to form several
safe and Commodious harbours'. He added:

*The Inhabitants of this Bay are far more numerous than any other
place we have yet been in and seem to live in friendship one with a
nother although it doth not att all appear that they are united under
one head. They inhabited both the Islands and the main and have a
number of Heppa's or strong holds, and these are all built upon such
a place as nature hath in a great part fortified and what she hath left
undone the people themselves have finished.*

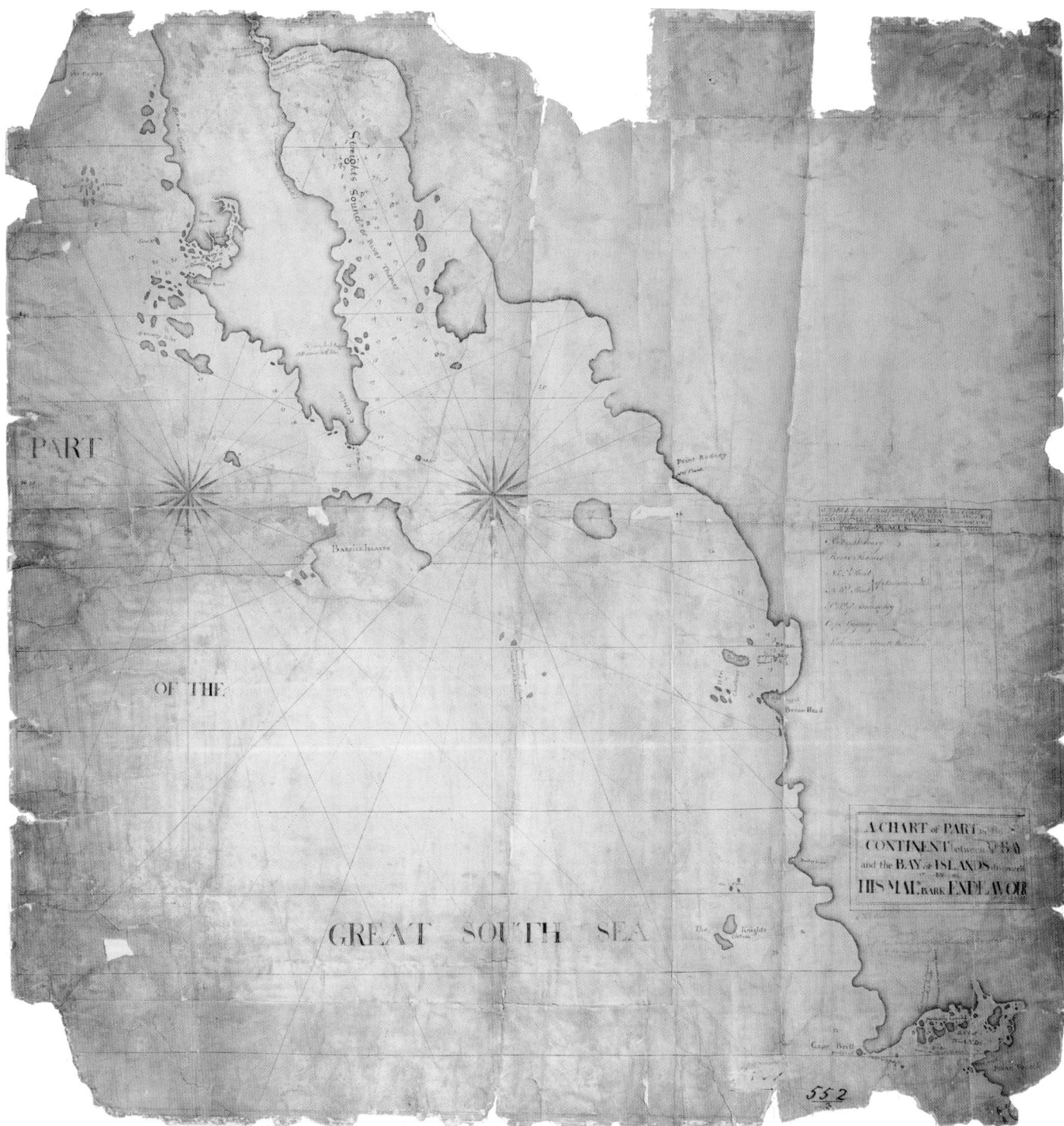

William Hodges (1744–1797)
Portrait of a Maori Chieftain 1773
Pictures Collection, National Library of Australia, Canberra,
PIC Drawer 9 #R747

In his journal, Georg Forster recorded the taking of this portrait at
Queen Charlotte Sound, on 22 October 1773:

*After breakfast three canoes put off from … the shore … in one of
them was a chief, who came on deck without hesitation. He was a tall
middle-aged man, clothed in two new and elegant dresses, made of the
New Zealand flag or flax and stuck with white feathers. In each ear
he wore a piece of albatross skin with its white down, and his face was
punctured in spirals and curved lines. Mr Hodges drew his portrait and
a print of it is inserted in Captain Cook's account of this voyage.*

William Hodges (1744–1797)
Woman of New Zealand 1773–75
Pictures Collection, National Library of Australia, Canberra,
PIC Drawer 8 #R740

Anders Sparrman, the Swedish naturalist on the second voyage,
records the making of this portrait—and gives his opinion freely:

*[Hodges] did not choose the most beautiful model as an example of
this country's female physiognomy … yet neither was this one of the
ugliest. What made the appearance of the women unpleasant was
their lips, which were often tattooed until they were blue … Language
difficulties at first gave rise to a misunderstanding between the girl and
the painter, for she, having been well paid to go down into the saloon,
imagined that she ought to give satisfaction … She was astonished
when signs were made for her to sit on a chair … to the wonderment
and entertainment of herself and the two savages with her, she quickly
saw her likeness appearing in a red crayon drawing.*

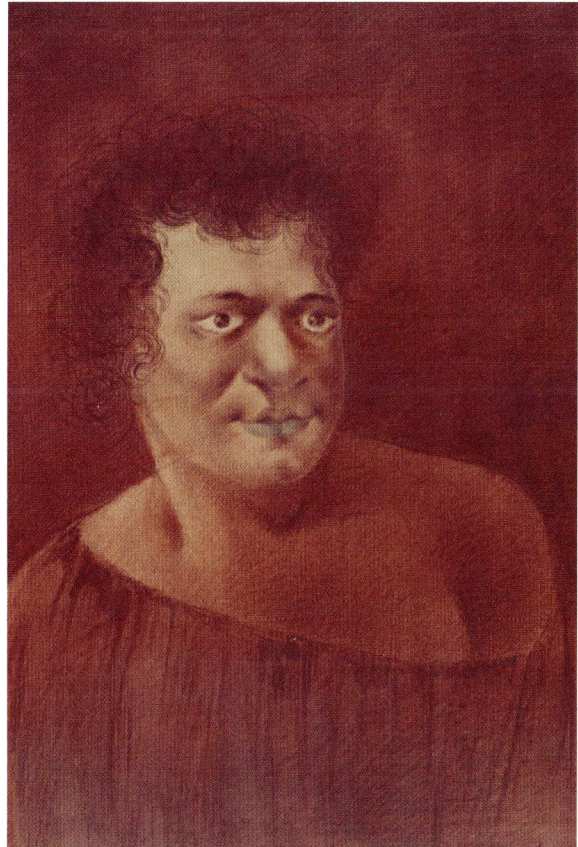

David Samwell (1751–1798)
Journal 1776–79
British Library, London, Egerton MS 2591, ff.12v–13r
© British Library Board

Samwell is best known to historians for his *Narrative of the Death of Cook* (1786). His journal includes Maori war songs, the haka, making it the most substantial record made of Maori language to that time.

These War Songs they call Ehaga, Several of which Taywheroos used to repeat to us the words are as follows, but we are quite at a loss for the meaning of them.

"Ehaga Toterannue"
or the War Song of New Zealand —

ahe ketaka paoure eta whaidanga nagoo Whāo è namaga tāware tana mea wagaw nghadia awite tebo pegira wahaw nghape kitanga ketaga teinoo ahaw kihei aw-whiw warawara katai maitepa eragi kahaw maitapaw heragi ahaw whā.

— Ehaga 2 —
Teira. temerama kaoure etepoi osagoo atooamati kaiti loginoo ewhage kinooana tearooa ketetahoo wagamanoo etaooa tengadoo owai pakooa etetoa ewhioo wireeira toò obogo, taboo kamatoo —

— Ehaga 3 —
agoo anai coaga tagodo iteka onodi odea ketoo katehoo wahooi pokia aiwroo tean mawo topea ooroo teama.

Ehaga 4

Rorongoo cowenaki nate hoowage neigedabo
eahooa tata tooge tetaw emahi meirooa
neimeawa cahe moitoa maiagooranje pahe-
wha hewa conohoteni coteta tapahi meikewar-
-ei cooroo pa anga maiewenoogoo eoohatata
toohooge tetaw emai mairooa neima hawa
cametoo.

Ehaga 5.

Tehitoo kihicoia wakahi tomonahoo hiahoo
kaietarego cainga pooga caria paira caw
pariaha kesetoogoo ketaga paouri waragi
tererenga awvaga adema Tangigi tehowa
iete naboora ee eho rerato nghadugi
tebooda ikai etiiva niwigi teahi ea

<u>a song of lamentation which
they sing at Burials</u>

Erooangaraw Haramainaia ketehooi toohoo
etimeiradoo ewainganooi oowagoo cawanganei
tootooaheni wagahiritidia keinoonomai
tekai ahoorahoo monaraweroo etaka
eirooa mahangana camitoo

Unknown artist after R. Ralph (artist)
after John Frederick Miller (artist, 1759–1796)
*A Chest of New Zealand, as a Specimen of the Carving
of That Country* 1773
Kerry Stokes Collection, Perth, 2012.070.3

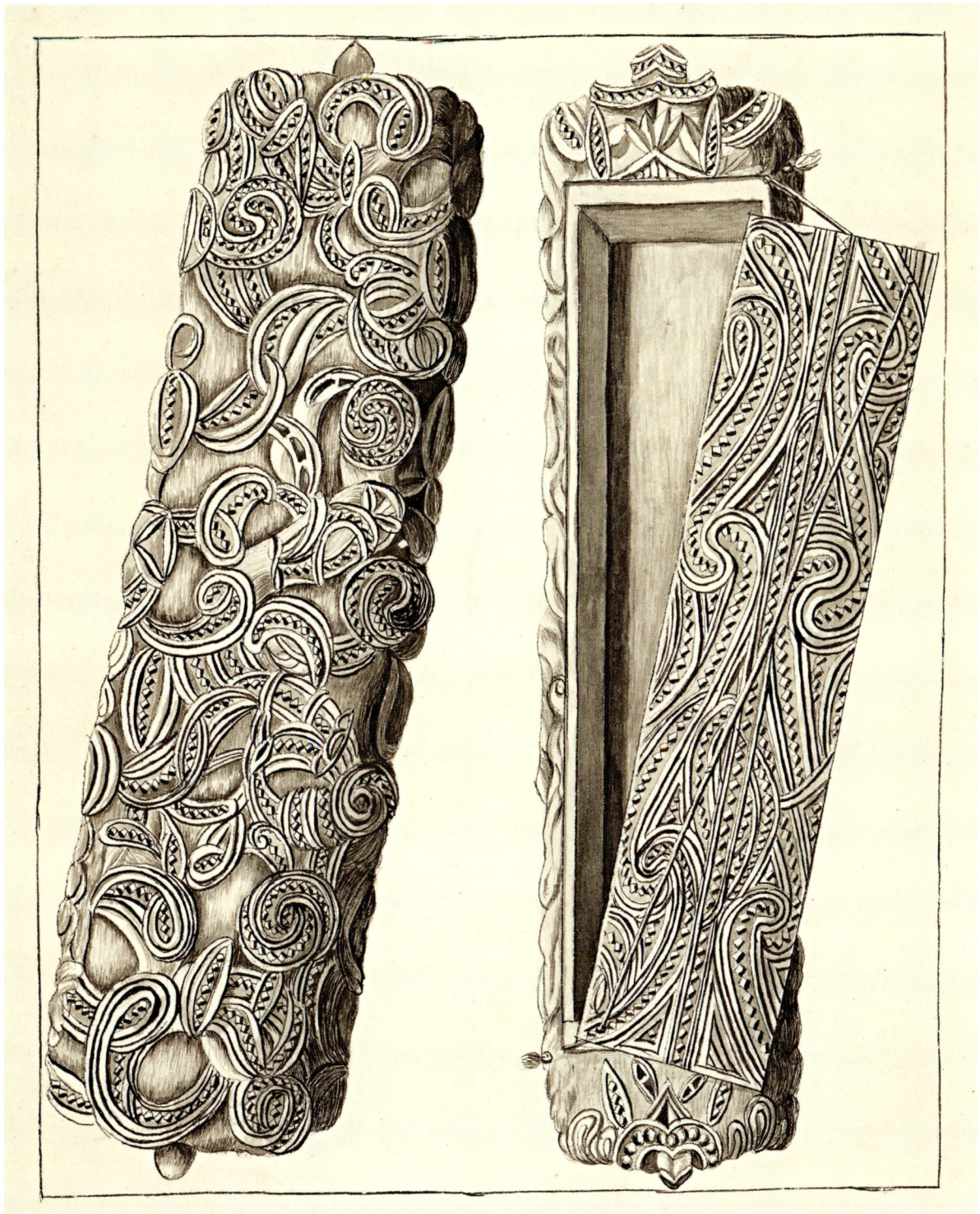

William Sharp (engraver, 1749–1824),
after John Webber (artist, 1752–1793)
A Night Dance by Men in Hapaee 1784
Rex Nan Kivell Collection (Pictures), National Library
of Australia, Canberra, PIC Drawer 87 #U1245 NK10975/5

On 20 May 1777, at Ha'apai in 'Otu Motu Anga 'Ofa (Tonga), Cook
and his men witnessed a series of dances by men and women. Artist
John Webber recorded these in a series of sketches and pen-and-
wash drawings, which were later engraved for the official account.
He created striking images of the Tongans and sailors watching the
performance on an equal footing.

Cook is shown in the centre foreground, talking to the Tongan man
to his right. He wrote of Webber's drawings of these dances that
they 'will give a very good idea of the order in which they range
themselves but neither pen nor pencil can describe the numerous
actions and motions they observe, which as I have before observed
are easy and graceful and many of them extremely so'.

'**As you can see here, Captain Cook and his crew from the**
Resolution **and the** ***Discovery*** **were treated to lavish feasting**
and magnificent entertainment. The warmth of the people
really came out. Their *talitali kakai* **(hospitality) and** *anga'ofa*
(generosity) were quite obvious to Captain Cook. Hence he gave
the name the Friendly Islands or 'Otu Motu Anga 'Ofa.'

Manutu'ufanga Naufahu, Tongan Community, Canberra

J. Webber del.

A NIGHT DANCE by MEN, in H.

Carved Ivory Female Figure from Tonga c. 1770
Australian Museum, Sydney, H000151–004

'This carved ivory image of a female was made for high-ranking women. The interesting thing now is that we do hold women in very high esteem. Women are very highly respected in our Tongan culture.'

Toa Fulivai Takiari, Tongan Community, Canberra

16

Wm Sharp sculp.

William Byrne (engraver, 1743–1805)
after William Hodges (artist, 1744–1797)
View in the Island of New Caledonia
London: Wm Strahan & Thos Cadell, 1777
Pictures Collection, National Library of Australia, Canberra,
PIC Drawer 10 #S1722

Sailing westward from the New Hebrides (Vanuatu) in September 1774, the *Resolution* anchored at Balade, on the north-east coast of a large island Cook named New Caledonia for its tall pines and mountains. The expedition journals and works of art are the earliest known description of New Caledonian society. Cook recorded: 'Balade was the Name of the district we were at and Tia Boma the Chief, he lived on the other side of the ridge of hills, so that we had but little of his Company and therefore could see but little of his power'. The high chiefs of Balade belonged to the Tea Bweon (or Tea Puma) clan, who lived near the present town of Ouégoa.

After an exchange of gifts, relations were generally good, though Cook sometimes misread the nature of the relationship. On one occasion, he and the two Forsters suffered a bout of poisoning after eating a 'fine large Fish' purchased from 'an Indian'. Even the 'evident Signs of aversion' later expressed towards it by several local inhabitants did not shake the Europeans' confidence in the good will of these people.

Drawn from Nature by W. Hodges.

VIEW IN THE ISLAND OF NEW C

TOP

William Hodges (1744–1797)
Man of New Caledonia 1774
Pictures Collection, National Library of Australia, Canberra,
PIC Drawer 12 #R754

BOTTOM

William Hodges (1744–1797)
Woman of New Caledonia 1774
Pictures Collection, National Library of Australia, Canberra,
PIC Drawer 11 #R750

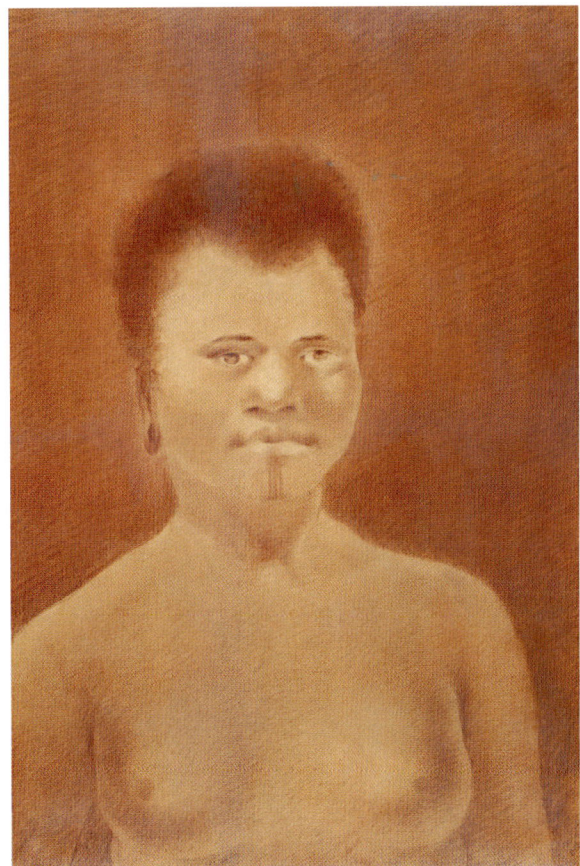

Engraved by W. Byrne.

NIA

William Woollett (engraver, 1735–1785),
after William Hodges (artist, 1744–1797)
Monuments in Easter Island
Pictures Collection, National Library of Australia, Canberra,
PIC Solander Box B14 #S1711

OPPOSITE TOP

William Hodges (1744–1797)
A Woman of Easter Island 1775
Pictures Collection, National Library of Australia, Canberra,
PIC Drawer 9 #R746

The *Resolution*'s visit to Easter Island in mid-March 1774 lasted
only three days. The visitors made particular note of the hats the
women wore. An Easter Island man took Hodges' hat—right off his
head. Astronomer William Wales records, with tongue in cheek, the
artist's philosophical attitude to the loss. He alludes to Shakespeare's
Twelfth Night: 'He sat like Patience on a Monument Smiling at Grief'.

Drawn from Nature by W. Hodges.

MONUMENTS IN EASTER ISL

Published Feb. 1.st 1777, by W. Strahan New Street Shoe Lane, & Tho.s Cadell in the S

BOTTOM

William Hodges (1744–1797)
Man of Easter Island 1775
Pictures Collection, National Library of Australia, Canberra,
PIC Drawer 8 #R741

The man depicted here was probably the one who visited the
Resolution. Wales described him this way:

*This man was of a middle height, rather slender and seemed to be
about 50 years of Age. His Complexion was of a dark Copper-Colour,
his Eyes a dark brown & his hair black and cut short … He appeared
very brisk and Active, and to take much notice of what was round
him … The pendant parts of his Ears had long slits in them, and were
extended to at least 2 Inches in length; when he saw us taking notice
of them, he turned the slits over the upper parts, so that at first look
it might have been conjectured the small flap had been cut away.*

Engraved by W. Woollett.
Nº XLIX.

John Keyes Sherwin (engraver, 1751–1790)
after William Hodges (artist, 1744–1797)
The Landing at Tanna, One of the New Hebrides
Pictures Collection, National Library of Australia, Canberra,
PIC Solander Box B14 #S1720

OPPOSITE TOP

William Hodges (1744-1797)
Man of Tanna 1774
Pictures Collection, National Library of Australia, Canberra,
PIC Drawer 11 #R752

The Melanesian people at Tanna were more receptive than those at
Niue and Erramango, where a fight broke out and four locals were
killed. The ship put in for repairs at what came to be called Port
Resolution, in August 1774, and the Forsters were able to venture
inland and observe people, settlements and agriculture.

Yet communication of words and gestures between Cook's party
and the Tannese remained superficial, and the relationship was
irreparably damaged when a sentry shot and killed a man.

Painted by W. Hodges.

The Landing at TANNA *one of the* NEW HI

Published Feb.º 1ˢᵗ 1777. by Wᵐ Strahan, New Street, Shoe Lane, & Thoˢ Cadell in the Stran

William Hodges (1744–1797)
Woman and Child of Tanna 1774
Pictures Collection, National Library of Australia, Canberra,
PIC Drawer 9 #R745

Naturalist Johann Reinhold Forster recorded:

> *The Women have all the same ornaments as Men, Nose–Stones,*
> *Earrings, Shells on the Breast & Bracelets … their heads covered*
> *with a kind of cap made of a Plantain leaf or a Mat–Basket. Few are*
> *uncovered, & ever very young Girls have these Caps. The women carry*
> *their young Children on their backs in a kind of bag made of a piece of*
> *cloth of the abovementioned kind.*

Engraved by I.K.Sherwin.

Drawn from Nature by W. Hodges.

THE ICE ISLANDS,

London, Publifh'd as the Act directs July 16. 1776.

Engrav'd by B.T. Pouncy.

Benjamin Thomas Pouncy (engraver, d. 1799),
after William Hodges (artist, 1744–1797)
The Ice Islands Seen on the 9th of Jany 1773
Pictures Collection, National Library of Australia, Canberra,
PIC Solander Box B14 #S1701

Cook crossed into the Antarctic Circle several times between
December 1772 and February 1774, going as far south as 71° 10'
latitude. He then undertook a number of sweeps of the Pacific,
proving there was no vast *Terra Australis*. In this engraving, the men
in the boat in the foreground are collecting ice to supplement the
ship's water supply.

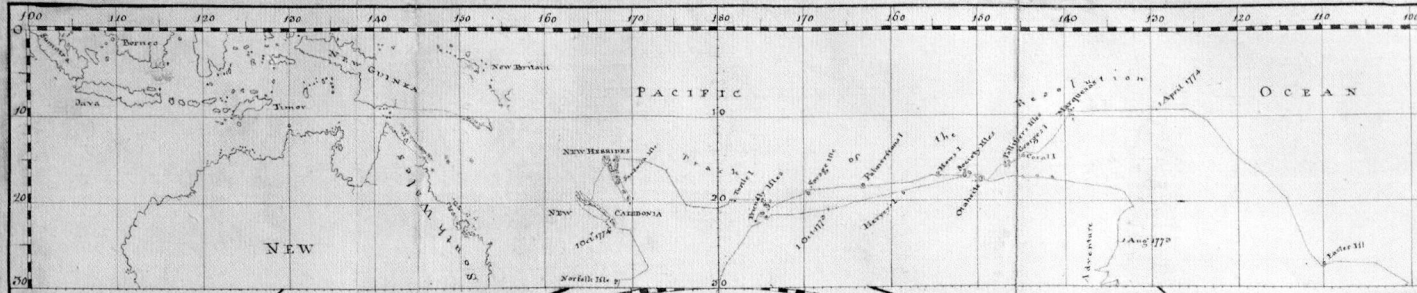

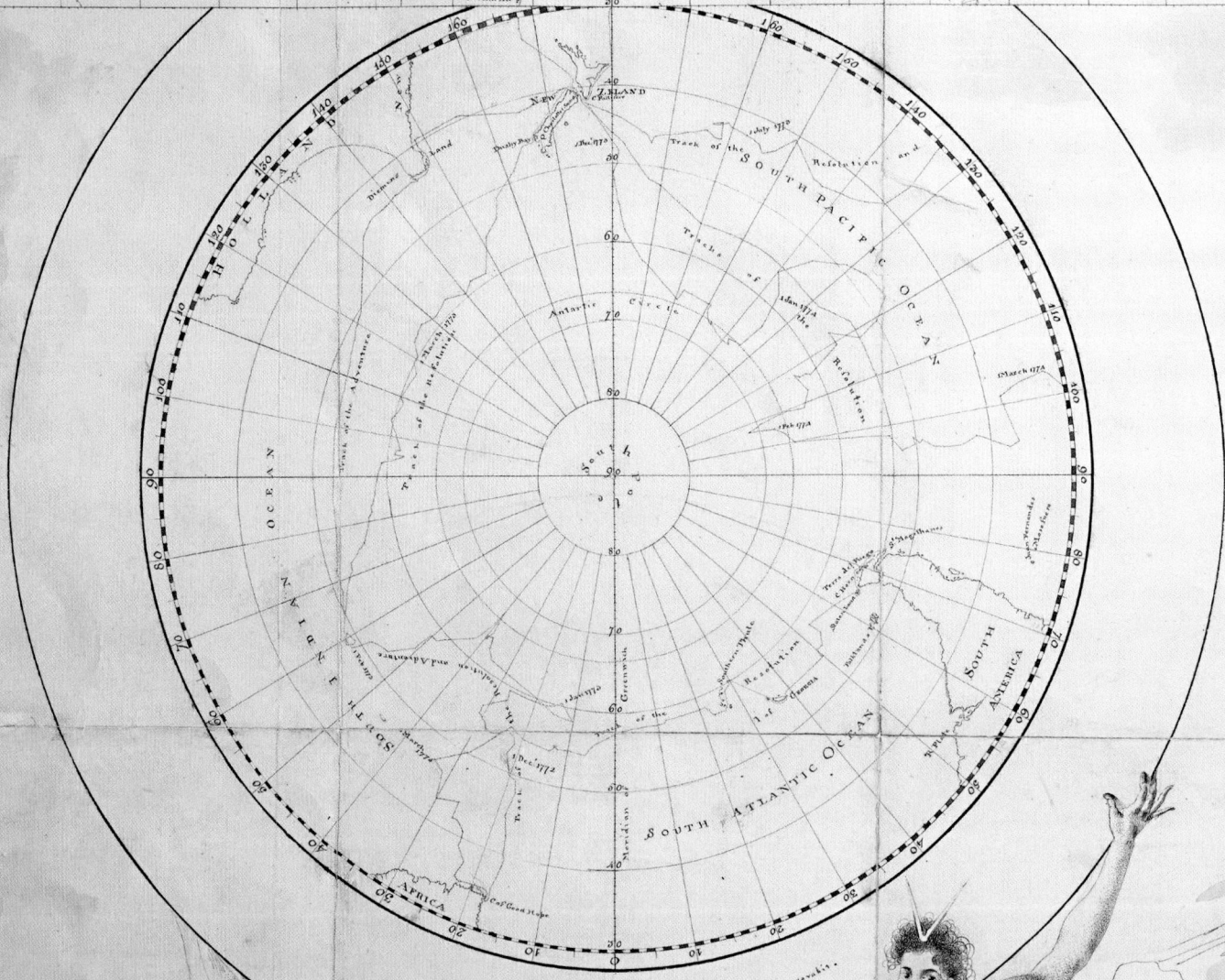

CHART
of the
SOUTHERN HEMISPHERE
Shewing the Track and
Discoveries made by the
RESOLUTION
under the Command of
J.s Cook.

James Cook (cartographer, 1728–1779),
Henry Roberts (cartographer, c.1757–1796)
and William Hodges (artist, 1744–1797)
*Chart of the Southern Hemisphere, Showing the Track and
Discoveries Made by the Resolution* c.1775
The National Archives, UK, ADM 55/108 f.1b
© Crown Copyright – image courtesy of The National Archives

This is an early version of the map produced at the end of the
second Pacific voyage. That Cook saw it as a summation of his
voyage's achievements is clear, as this map was the frontispiece to the
copy of his journal sent back to the Admiralty from Cape Town.

It is also a statement on the collaborative nature of Cook's voyages—
the bringing together of Cook's and Roberts' mapping, Hodges'
figures and Forster's quotation in one map.

The drawing includes a track chart of the *Resolution*'s voyage in
the South Pacific, in addition to a south polar view. The world
is supported by allegorical figures representing Labour (left)
and Science (right). Just above their heads is a Latin quotation,
modified for this map by the naturalist Johann Reinhold Forster,
from the second book of Virgil's great epic poem, *The Aeneid*.
It can be translated thus: 'For though Labour supports the globe
with the utmost exertion of power, Science seems to do it with
great Ease.'

William Hodges (1744–1797)
Head of a Maori Man c. 1775
Petherick Collection (Pictures), National Library of Australia,
Canberra, PIC Drawer 7 #R139

This drawing is thought to be a study for the allegorical figure of
Labour in the chart at left.

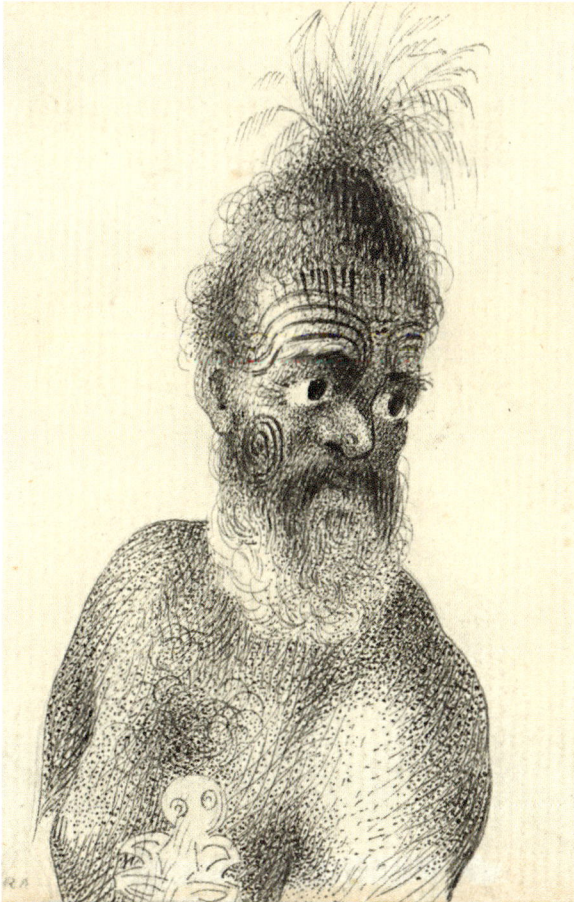

5. NEW HOLLAND

After mapping New Zealand in 1770, Cook had to decide which way to go home. The Admiralty's secret instructions required him to search for the fabled 'Great South Land'. The majority of the territory we now know as Australia had been mapped by the Dutch in the seventeenth century, and Cook knew these maps well. The east coast and parts of Tasmania, however, were still uncharted on European maps. Ever eager for a challenge, Cook decided to return via what he believed to be the east coast of New Holland, and therefore fill the void on Europe's maps. He wrote in his journal that he was inclined 'to bend my thoughts towards returning home by such a rout as might conduce most to the advantage of the service I am upon, I consulted with the officers upon the most eligible way of putting this in execution'. This would allow him to meet the country's people, of whom he was aware from William Dampier's popular 1697 account.

That Cook's ships visited Australia on all three of his Pacific voyages is not well known. The most exhaustive visit was the *Endeavour*'s passage northwards up the east coast between April and August 1770. On the second voyage, the *Adventure* spent time in Van Diemen's Land, which was visited again on the third voyage by both the *Resolution* and the *Discovery*. The local people managed the land in ways unknown to, and mostly unseen by, the Europeans, who were also unaware of their rich oral traditions. There were few interactions between Cook's men and the Indigenous Australians; communication was difficult and sometimes misunderstandings led to violence. However, the native flora and fauna encountered by the Europeans during the *Endeavour* voyage were much more comprehensively observed, collected and documented.

James Cook (1728–1779)
A Chart of New South Wales, or the East Coast
of New-Holland (detail) 1773
London: W. Strahan & T. Cadell
Maps Collection, National Library of Australia, Canberra,
MAP T 325

This engraving of Cook's chart of the east coast of Australia
appeared in John Hawkesworth's 1773 account of the *Endeavour*
voyage. It tracks the voyage from Point Hicks in the south to
the 'Endeavours Streights' (Torres Strait) in the north, and shows
the places where the ship anchored. Cook named many coastal
features, sometimes explaining his reasoning in his journal.

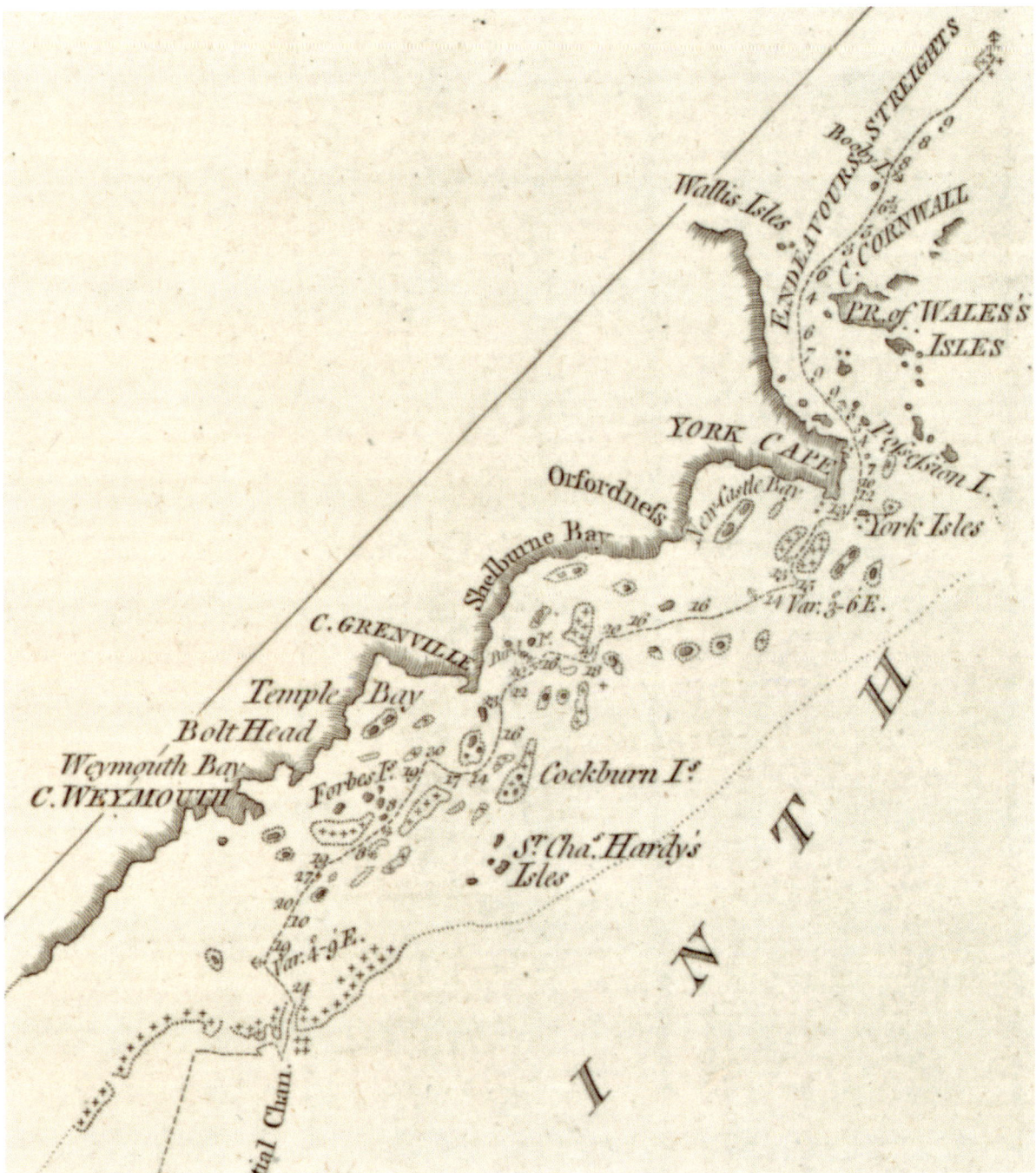

Charles Praval (copyist, d.1821), after a voyage artist
Views of Lands on the Coast of New South Wales 1770–71
British Library, London, Add MS 7085, f.36 b, c, e
© British Library Board

By the time of Cook's Pacific voyages, it was customary to produce coastal profiles as navigational aids. They showed what landmarks looked like from a ship, turning marks on a map into recognisable landscapes. Charles Praval, who joined the *Endeavour* voyage at Batavia in 1770, made copies of works for inclusion in the voyage's official graphic record.

'My people have lived in this area for millennia. Pigeon House, or Didthul as we call it, is a very sacred place to us. It has men's sites and women's sites; it has art sites. It is not a site that we visit constantly, but it is a place that we hold very dear to our heart. It was also very well known outside our area and is also a very sacred place for other Aboriginal people who live both north, south and west of us.'

Shane Carriage, Murramarang, Ulladulla, NSW

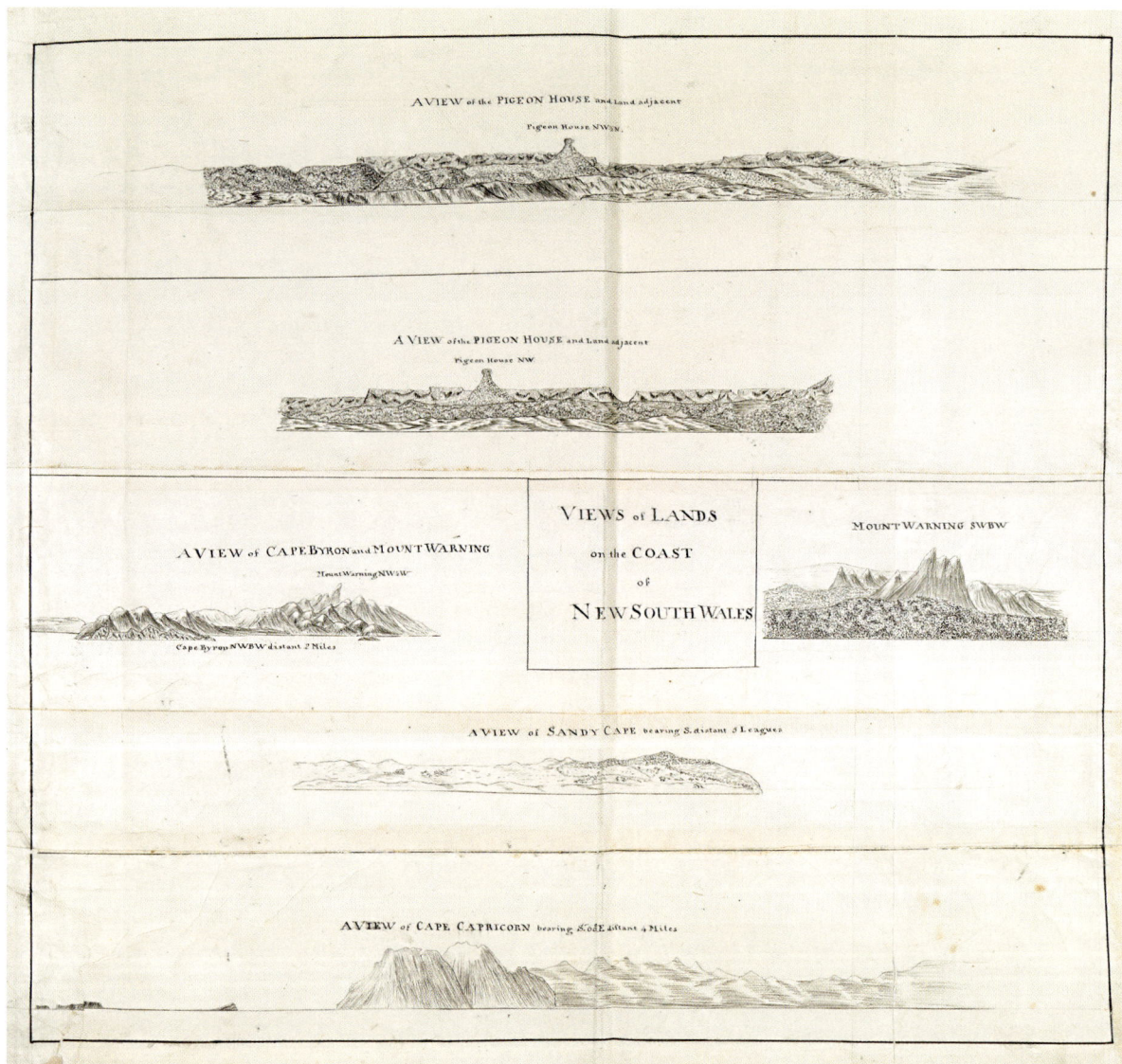

Richard Pickersgill (1749–1779)
Remarks on the Coast of New Holland in
Journal 7 October 1769 – 20 August 1770
The National Archives, UK, ADM 51/4547, ff.63v–64r
© Crown Copyright – image courtesy of The National Archives

The journal of Richard Pickersgill, master on the *Endeavour* voyage, records in simple language what the men aboard ship saw as they sailed northward along the coast. For example, on 21 and 22 April 1770 they 'saw a remarkable peaked hill with a tuft of toll tress on the resembling the top of a Pidgeon house … Mod[erate] and Pleasant W[eathe]r saw some smooks on shore … as we stood along shore we saw 4 of 5 of the Indians sitting … [by] the fire they appeard Naked and very black which was all we could discerne at that Distce'.

For nearly a decade, Pickersgill was almost continuously at sea. He had sailed with Captain Samuel Wallis's *Dolphin* voyage (1766–68) and later embarked on Cook's second Pacific voyage as a third lieutenant. Cook had a high opinion of Pickersgill. He was given command of a ship in 1776, but it went badly and he became an alcoholic. Pickersgill drowned in the Thames in 1779, aged 30.

'A lot of the knowledge that we hold is not knowledge that's found in books. A lot of the knowledge that we've got comes down from our Aboriginal ancestors all passed on through generations and generations. We talk about our local sites Didthul (Pigeon House). Places like that are part of our songlines, they connect the mountains to the sea.'

Victor Channell, Murramarang, Ulladulla, NSW

Richard Pickersgill (1749–1779)
A Plan of Sting-ray Bay on the E[as]t Coast of New Holland 1770
The National Archives, UK, ADM 352/383
© Crown Copyright – image courtesy of The National Archives

The *Endeavour* voyage journals and maps reveal that Cook's first name for Botany Bay was 'Sting-ray Bay', after the rays they caught there. In his journal entry for 5 May 1770, Pickersgill describes the bay:

> it is form'd by two Low pts: between which there is a Passage of one mile with fm water on the Et –side lies a Little Island and off the So

end of it is a shore where the sea sometimes Breakes after you are in the Bay spreads and tends to the Wt ward for about 6 or 7 Miles and then ends in two large Lagoons off the ... lies large flats with only 6 & 7 feet water upon them is a great Quantity of Stingerrays.

Cook had a high opinion of Pickersgill as a surveyor, and his maps provide an interesting stylistic contrast to the better-known maps by Cook and Isaac Smith used to illustrate the official voyage account.

Herman Diedrich Spöring (1733–1771)
Finished Pencil Drawing of Urolophus testaceus 1770
Natural History Museum, London, Drawing No. 50

Around 300 zoological drawings were made on the *Endeavour*
voyage, by three men—Sydney Parkinson, Alexander Buchan
and Herman Spöring—all of whom died on the voyage. Spöring,
a Swedish/Finnish naturalist, completed six drawings of sting rays,
all at Botany Bay. His surviving works are very precise. At the bottom
of the drawing is a detail of the underside of the head of the ray;
the annotations below that refer to another ray

RAJA testacea.

Sydney Parkinson (1745–1771)
Two Australian Aboriginal People and Other Drawings
April 1770 in *Sketchbook* 1768–71
British Library, London, Add MS 9345, f.14v
© British Library Board

This field sketch, Parkinson's most significant surviving drawing of Australian Aboriginal people, may date to 28 April 1770, when the *Endeavour* was at Botany Bay. In his journal, he writes:

> *Their canoes were made of one piece of bark, gathered at two ends, and extended in the middle by two sticks. Their paddles were very small, two of which they used at one time … After we had landed, they threw two of their lances at us; one of which fell between my feet … some … were painted white, having a streak round their thighs, two below their knees, one like a sash over their shoulders, which ran diagonally downwards, and another across their foreheads.*

Tupaia (c. 1724–1770)
Australian Aboriginal People in Bark Canoes April 1770
British Library, London, Add MS 15508, f.10
© British Library Board

In his journal for 28 April 1770, Banks described a scene which
could have inspired this work:

*By noon we were within the mouth of the inlet which appeard to be
very good. Under the South head of it were four small canoes; in each
of these was one man who held in his hand a long pole with which he
struck fish, venturing with his little imbarkation almost into the surf.
These people seemd to be totaly engag'd in what they were about: the
ship passd within a quarter of a mile of them and yet they scarce lifted
their eyes from their employment; I was almost inclind to think that
attentive to their business and deafned by the noise of the surf they
neither saw nor heard her go past them.*

This is one of a series of distinctive drawings found among Sir
Joseph Banks' collections, originally attributed to Banks. In the
1990s, a reference in Banks' voluminous correspondence made
it clear that the Ra'iatean navigator Tupaia had himself drawn one,
and therefore presumably all the other similar works in that series.
Tupaia joined the *Endeavour* voyage at Tahiti, and played a pivotal
role as an intermediary, translator and navigator, particularly in
New Zealand. He died of scurvy in Batavia in November 1770.

Boomerangs c. 1770
Australian Museum, Sydney, H000313 and H000314

There has been much debate over the years about whether the men of the *Endeavour* saw or collected boomerangs while they travelled up Australia's east coast. The journals contain references to Aboriginal weapons that seem similar, but surviving drawings of the ones collected on the voyage do not include any boomerangs. In terms of their provenance, these boomerangs and clubs have been associated with the *Endeavour* voyage.

Club c. 1770
Australian Museum, Sydney, H000294

Charles Praval (d. 1821)
Portrait of an Australian Aboriginal Person c. 1770–71
British Library, London, Add MS 15508, f.15
© British Library Board

This is believed to be a copy of a lost original by Sydney Parkinson. Some scholars have argued that it depicts a man from the Endeavour River area.

'We have a special story to tell, because when Captain Cook came here in 1770 to repair his ship, he didn't realise he had landed on a neutral zone. This Clan Land of Waymburr was a place where women from surrounding Clans came to give birth, marriage alliances were made here, conflicts were settled here. Bama came here for initiation ceremonies, for celebrations. The law said that there was no blood to be spilt on this *bubu* on this land. Not many people know that without the cultural and spiritual laws of the Guugu Yimithirr Bama, Cook would not have had a successful first voyage.'

Alberta Hornsby, Guugu Yimithirr, Cooktown, QLD

CH·PRAVAL DEL·

John Frederick Miller (1759–1796)
*Five Spears and a Shield from New Zealand, Australia and
New Guinea* 1771
British Library, London, Add MS 23920, f.35
© British Library Board

After the *Endeavour* returned to London, Miller was employed by
Banks to draw objects collected on the voyage. This is the most
detailed depiction of the only shield that can definitely be said to
have been collected in New Holland during the *Endeavour* voyage.
Whether the shield itself survives is unclear.

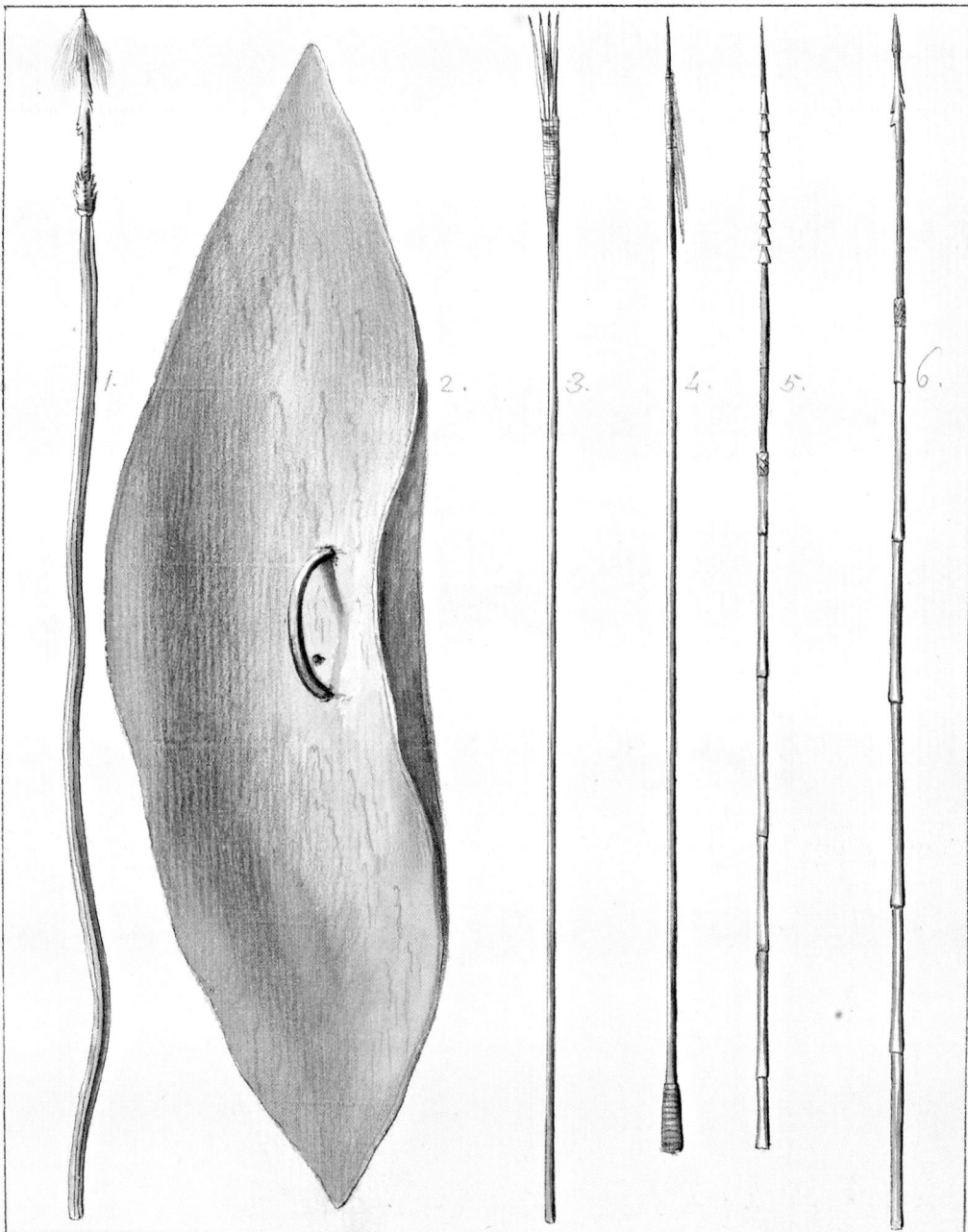

Richard Pickersgill (1749–1779)
A Plan of the River on the East Coast of New Holland Where HM Bark Endeavour Repaired Her Bottom After Running on a Reef of Rocks Where She Lay 24 Hours 1770
The National Archives, UK, ADM 352/381
© Crown Copyright – image courtesy of The National Archives

On 11 June 1770 the *Endeavour* struck a coral reef. Though this was a major disaster, the time required for repairs had the advantage of forcing an extended stay in the area, which allowed for a more meaningful interaction with, and observation of, the local environment. Drawn after repairs to the *Endeavour* had been effected, it shows the coastline, the tidal section of the Endeavour River and details the shoals and sand bars, mangroves and 'Good Fishing Ground'. The *Endeavour* was hauled ashore at point 'B'.

Sydney Parkinson (1745–1771)
Unfinished Pencil Sketch of a Green Turtle (Chelonia mydas)
Endeavour River 1770
Natural History Museum, London, Drawing No. 43

Green turtles were, and continue to be, important to the Guugu Yimithirr people of Waalumbaal Birri (Endeavour River). In 1770 they were present in abundance (in his notes, called 'slip books', botanist Daniel Solander notes that the turtles were breeding in July–August), and the men of the *Endeavour* caught and ate a great many of them.

On 18–19 July groups of Guugu Yimithirr people came aboard, and saw how many turtles the men of the *Endeavour* had taken. Cook writes about the second visit, 'those that came on board were very desirous of having our turtle'. Prevented from retrieving any, the Guugu Yimithirr set fires on land, killing an *Endeavour* sow and piglets. Cook responded by firing a musket, wounding a ringleader.

The Guugu Yimithirr returned with, as Cook put it, '4 or 5 darts a piece'. The British took some of these from them and followed them; then, at an outcrop of igneous rocks now called Reconciliation Rocks, as Banks relates, 'the little old man now came forward to us carrying a lance without a point … he then spoke to the others'. Cook goes on to describe how 'after some unintelligible conversation had pass'd they lay down their darts and came to us in a very friendly manner; we now returnd the darts we had taken from them which reconciled every thing'. The Guugu Yimithirr people today consider this 'the first recorded reconciliation between Indigenous and non-indigenous people in Australia'.

James Cook (1728–1779)
Journal of HMB Endeavour 1768–71
Manuscripts Collection, National Library of Australia,
Canberra, MS 1 f.256r
Inscribed on the UNESCO Memory of the World Register, 2001

Purchased by the Australian government for the nation in 1923 for £5,000, this manuscript journal in Cook's own hand is often considered a foundational treasure of the National Library of Australia. Cook's clerk, Richard Orton, made a copy of it that was submitted to the Admiralty at the end of the voyage. This is the version Cook chose to keep. It is still a draft, though a fair copy, with various crossings-out and amendments, which show careful rethinking and reworking on the part of its author. The journal is all the more important as Cook had very little control over the publication of the official printed account of the voyage, which was edited by John Hawkesworth.

This is one of most visually exciting pages of the entire journal. It records the tense days in mid-June 1770 after the *Endeavour* struck the reef, and what the men did to salvage it. One sentence encapsulates the emotion of this time: 'A Mistake soon after happened which for the first time caused fear to operate upon every man in the Ship.'

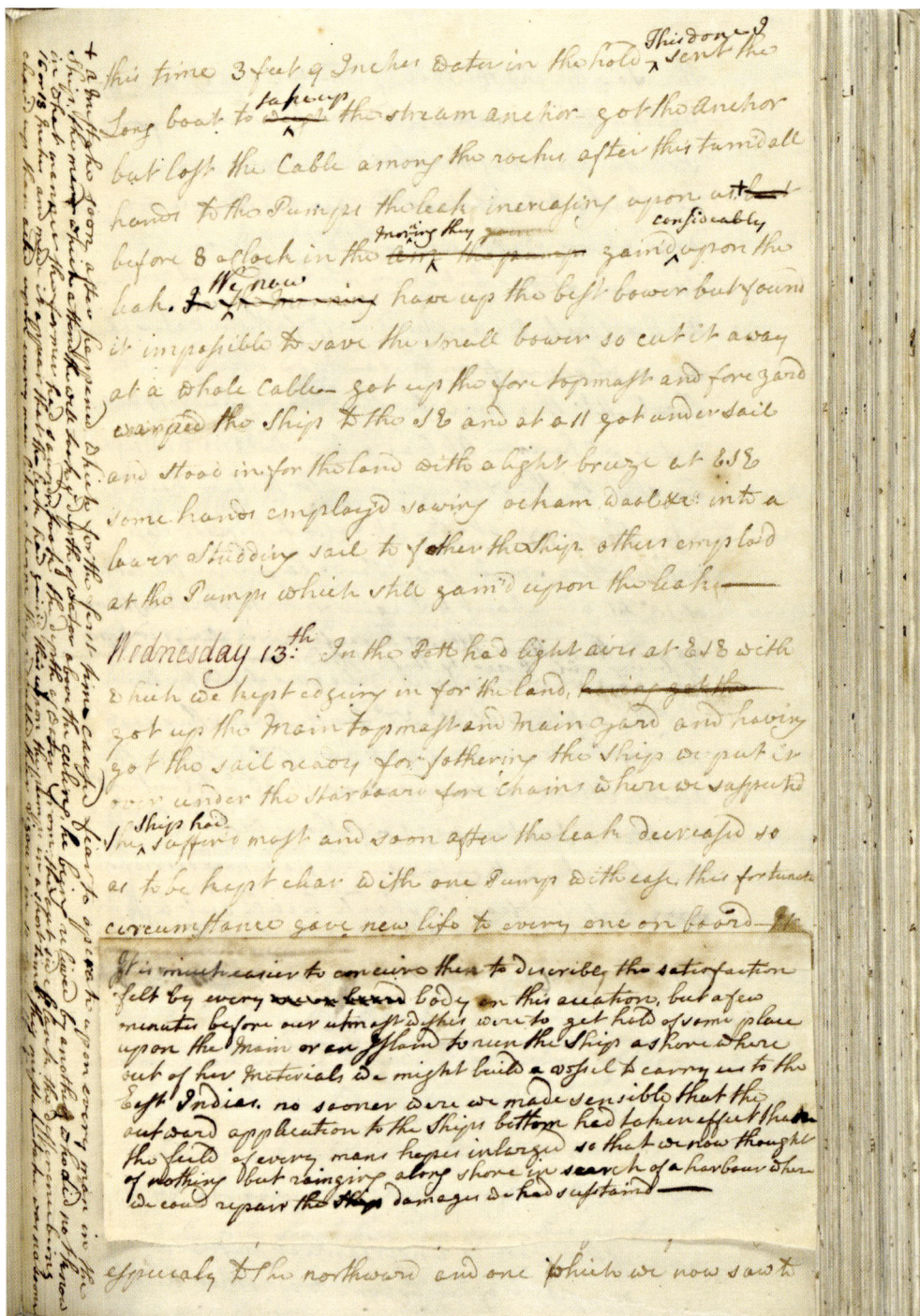

Richard Orton (copyist), after James Cook (author, 1728–1779)
Endeavour Journal Submitted to the Admiralty at the End of the Voyage 1771
The National Archives, UK, ADM 55/40 ff.142v–143r
© Crown Copyright – image courtesy of The National Archives

This official copy of Cook's own *Endeavour* journal, written in the hand of his clerk, was submitted to the Admiralty at the end of the voyage. As might be expected, the corresponding passages for these June days at Endeavour River convey none of the drama of Cook's original journal. It is possible that this is the first time these two versions of Cook's *Endeavour* journal have been reunited since the 1770s.

(264) *New South Wales or*   *the East Coast of New Holland.* (265)   143

Official Log of the Endeavour 1768–71 (detail)
British Library, London, Add MS 8959, f.130v
© British Library Board

The official log of the *Endeavour* voyage records how on 22 August 1770 'at 6 Possession was taken of this Country in his majesty's Name & under his Coulours Fired several volleys of small arms on the occasion & Cheer'd 3 times which was answerd from the ship'. In his journal, Cook could be more descriptive. After satisfying himself that they had reached the northern limit of the land and were about to pass through a 'Passage' [Torres Strait], he then honoured the Dutch navigators and took possession 'of the whole eastern coast … by the name of *New South Wales*'. Cook added, 'We saw on all the Adjacent Lands and Islands a great number of smooks, a certain sign that they are Inhabited, and we have dayly seen smooks on every part of the coast we have lately been upon'.

Endeavour Muster Book 1768–72
The National Archives, UK, ADM 36/8569, ff.185v–186r (detail)
© Crown Copyright – image courtesy of The National Archives

A muster book was a key part of the official record-keeping aboard ship. Pay, deaths, desertions, additional crew members—all are recorded. These pages record the pay given between December 1770 and January 1771 to what were called 'supernumeraries', that is, men not in the employ of the navy. They include Joseph Banks, Daniel Solander, astronomer Charles Green and his servant, voyage artist Sydney Parkinson, assistant naturalist Herman Spöring, and Tupaia ('Tupia, Native of Polinesia') and his servant Tarheto. All but Banks and Solander died around this time, most as a result of dysentery contracted at Batavia, where the *Endeavour* underwent repairs. Also listed here are men who joined the voyage at Batavia, including 'Chas Provall' (Charles Praval).

In his journal entry for 26 December 1770, Cook writes:

The Number sick on board … amounts to 40 or up wards and the rest of the Ships company are in a Weakly condition … But notwithstanding this general sickness we lost but Seven Men in the whole the Surgeon three Seamen, Mr Greens Servant and Tupia and his servant both of which fell a sacrifice to this unwholsom climate before they had reached the Object of their wishes … [Tupaia] was a Shrewd Sensible, Ingenious Man, but proud and obstinate which often made his situation on board both disagreeable to himself and those about him and tended much to promote the deceases which put a period to his life.

103

William Ellis (c. 1756–1785)
View of Adventure Bay, Van Diemen's Land, New Holland 1777
Pictures Collection, National Library of Australia, Canberra,
PIC Solander Box C16 #R11282

On the third Pacific voyage, the *Resolution* and *Discovery* spent about
a week restocking supplies in Adventure Bay, just off the east coast of
Tasmania, in late January 1777. In his entry for Monday 27 January,
Cook records 'altho' we had as yet seen none of the Inhabitants we
however saw their smoaks but a little way up in the woods'.

OPPOSITE

Resolution and Adventure Medal (the Killora Example) 1772
Private Collection

In 1914 a four-year-old girl, Janet Cadell, found this medal on a farm
at Killora on Bruny Island, Tasmania. It had been struck in 1772, as
a token to foster good relations with those Indigenous people Cook
came into contact with. Such medals were taken on both the second
and third Pacific voyages, and it is quite possible this particular one
was given out on either voyage.

On Wednesday 29 January 1777, Cook was with 'the wooding
party', and saw 'several of the Natives were … stroling along the
shore. We had not be long landed before about twenty of them men
and boys joined us without expressing the least fear or distrust,
some of them were same as had been with us the day before, but
the greatest part were strangers.' He noted the 'wit and humour'
of a 'humpbacked' man, but 'we regreted much that we could not
understand him for their language was wholy unintelligible to
us: it is different from that spoken by the inhabitants of the more
Northern parts of this Country … I gave each of them a string
of Beads and a Medal, which I thought they received with some
satisfaction.' This medal is the only example to appear in Australia
since then.

View of Adventure Bay, Van Die[...]

Land, New-Holland.

W: Ellis fec.t 1777

John Webber (1752–1793)
An Opossum of Van Diemen's Land c. 1782
pencil, pen, wash and watercolour
Rex Nan Kivell Collection (Pictures), National Library
of Australia, Canberra, PIC Drawer 84 #T432 NK52/1

One of the first European images of a ringtail possum (*Pseudocheirus peregrinus*), this is no doubt based on the possum shot at Adventure Bay, Van Diemen's Land, on 29 December 1776. This version of the work was clearly done, however, with a focus on the landscape, in preparation for its engraving for inclusion in the official voyage account, finally published in 1784. The State Library of New South Wales holds in its collection a version, dating to 1779, that gives the detail of the possum.

OPPOSITE

James Caldwall (engraver, 1739–1820),
after John Webber (artist, 1752–1793)
Proof of 'A Man of Van Diemen's Land', Annotated by John Webber c. 1784
Pictures Collection, National Library of Australia, Canberra, PIC Volume 564 #PIC/16904/11

Late on 27 January 1777, Cook met some of the local inhabitants, as he observed in his journal:

In the afternoon we were agreeably surprised at the place where we were cutting Wood, with a Visit from some of the Natives, Eight men and a boy: they came out of the Woods to us without shewing the least mark of fear and with the greatest confidence imaginable, for none of them had any weapons, except one who had in his hand a stick about 2 feet long and pointed at one end. They were quite naked & wore no ornaments, except the large punctures or ridges raised on the skin, some in straight and others in curved lines, might be reckoned as such: they were of the common stature but rather slenders; their skin was black and also their hair, which was as woolly as any Native of Guinea.

Caldwell

A Man of Van Diemans Land. New Holland.

Moses Griffiths pinx.^t 1772.

Moses Griffith (1747–1819)
Rainbow Lorikeet 1772
Pictures Collection, National Library of Australia, Canberra,
PIC Drawer 12822 #15600

This is the earliest known European coloured painting of an
Australian bird. The artist, Moses Griffith, was the servant and
painter of natural historian Thomas Pennant and often called on to
illustrate Pennant's works of natural history. Pennant called him an
'untaught genius, drawn from the most remote and obscure parts of
North Wales'. The bird depicted here is believed to be one Tupaia
had kept as a pet. It returned alive to England with the *Endeavour*,
and later became the property of Marmaduke Tunstall, a collector
and friend of Pennant.

Thomas Pennant (1726–1798)
*Animals Observed or Collected by Joseph Banks Esqr. & Doctor
Solander in the Voyage Round the World Begun August 25th 1768
Ended July 12th 1771* 1771–80s
Manuscripts Collection, National Library of Australia, Canberra,
MS 9138, f.21r

On his return, Banks appears to have passed his bird specimens
on to his close friend Pennant. In this working notebook, Pennant
collates descriptions of, and information about, animals seen on
the *Endeavour* voyage. He updated it in subsequent years to include
birds and animals seen on Cook's later voyages. Many pages are
struck through in pencil.

Myrtaceae Callistemon citrinus, Collected on the Endeavour Voyage at Botany Bay 1770
The Royal Botanic Gardens and Domain Trust, National Herbarium of New South Wales, Sydney, NSW133462

OPPOSITE

Proteaceae Grevillea pteridifolia, Collected on the Endeavour Voyage near Endeavour River 1770
The Royal Botanic Gardens and Domain Trust, National Herbarium of New South Wales, Sydney, NSW133650

On the Cook voyages extraordinary quantities of botanical and zoological specimens were collected. It is estimated, for example, that over 30,000 botanical specimens and over 1,000 zoological species were collected on the *Endeavour* voyage.

Of the botanical species, about 1,400 were unknown to Europeans before the voyage. The surviving journals also reflect that diligent approach to collecting, with many entries recording Banks and Solander 'botanising' on the voyage. Solander had trained under the great Swedish zoologist and taxonomist Carl Linnaeus. He continued to work for Banks after the voyage. Banks's herbarium eventually entered the British Museum. In the late nineteenth and early twentieth centuries, duplicates of the botanical specimens, having been transferred to the newly established Natural History Museum in London, were distributed to various botanical collections. These two examples came to Sydney; though they have been 'rehoused' they retain much of their original labelling, thereby revealing the hands they have passed through since being picked at Botany Bay and Endeavour River in 1770.

NATIONAL HERBARIUM OF N.S.W.
Callistemon citrinus (curtis) Skeels
DET. B.M. Wiecek   Aug 1993

...TIONAL HERBARIUM OF N.S.W.

...idifolia Knight
...e ISOLECTOTYPE
...eston   11 Oct 2013

...AL HERBARIUM OF NEW SOUTH WALES,
BOTANIC GARDENS, SYDNEY.
_____◆_____

Grevillea chrysodendra, R. Br.

QLD
N.S.W.

Date

NATIONAL HERBARIUM OF N.S.W.

Grevillea **pteridifolia Knight**
Probably parts of the type collections.
DETERMINAVIT D. J. McGillivray _____ McG. 1983

NSW133650

Ex Herbario Musei Britannici.

NEW HOLLAND

BANKS & SOLANDER
1770
Grevillea pteridifolia Kn.
Illustr. Bot. Cook's Voyage, tab. 261 P. 83

Sydney Parkinson (1745–1771)
Original Sketch with Colour Reference of Grevillea pteridifolia 1770
Natural History Museum, London, Cat. No. A7/317

To the young Quaker draughtsman Sydney Parkinson fell the task
of documenting botanical specimens collected on the voyage. In
a letter his friend Dr John Fothergill, Banks wrote that Parkinson
'with unbounded industry made for me a much larger number
of drawings than I ever expected'. In total, Parkinson completed
674 drawings and 269 watercolours. The sheer amount collected
defeated even him, and he died before he could complete
watercolours of specimens collected in New Holland. He had,
however, focused on finishing pencil sketches (such as this one),
with colours noted, before the specimens degraded.

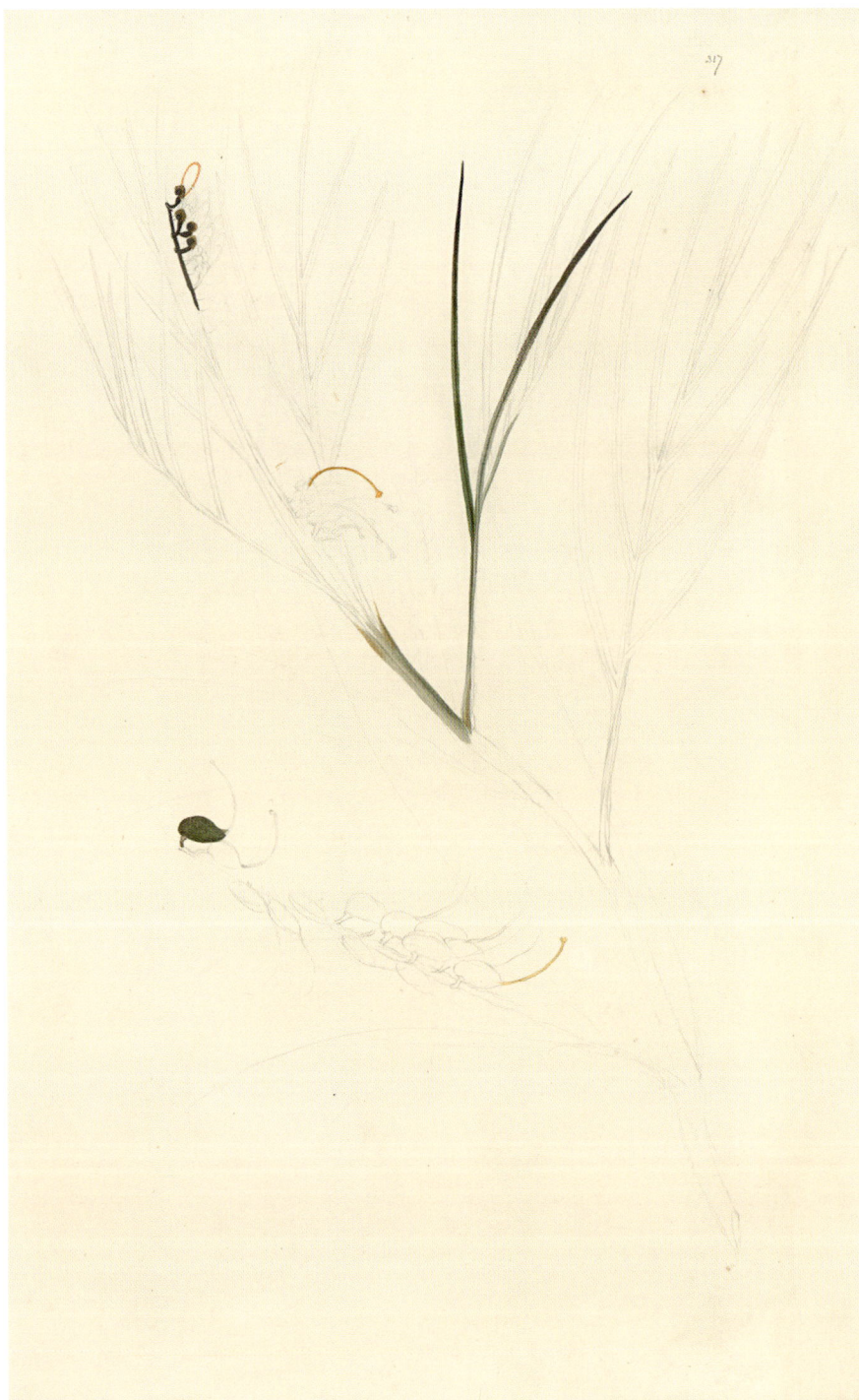

John Frederick Miller (artist, 1759–1796),
after Sydney Parkinson (artist, 1745–1771)
Finished Watercolour of Grevillea pteridifolia 1770s
Natural History Museum, London, Cat. No. A7/317

Copperplate Engraving of Grevillea pteridifolia c. 1774–84
Natural History Museum, London, Cat. No. A7/317

From 1773 to 1784 Joseph Banks led and funded an ambitious program whose aim was to produce printed volumes of colour illustrations, of specimens collected on the *Endeavour* voyage. Artists such the illustrator John Frederick Miller (1759–1796) completed the work Sydney Parkinson had been unable to, turning his pencil sketches into completed watercolours. In all, 18 engravers cut 738 copperplates, ready for printing. For various reasons, however, only proof prints were printed. In the 1980s, Editions Alecto, in association with the Natural History Museum, conserved these eighteenth-century plates, and made prints from them, in an ambitious project whose result is popularly known as *Banks' Florilegium.*

6. NORTH PACIFIC

Towards the end of his second Pacific voyage, Cook felt he had exhausted what he could do in the Southern hemisphere, describing it on 21 February 1775 as 'sufficiently explored'. Indeed, on his return to England, it was widely expected that he would spend his remaining days in semi-retirement. As it turned out, he was soon considering an expedition to find the fabled Northwest Passage. This supposed route between the Pacific and Atlantic oceans would present enormous trading advantages if found, and so it became the aim of his third Pacific voyage, which set off in July 1776.

Every bit as extraordinary as the previous two voyages, it was a highly ambitious venture, and one that ended with Cook's death. Cook again took the *Resolution* and another Whitby collier, the *Discovery*, through the by now familiar Pacific routes towards north-western America, chancing on Hawaii in January 1778. Those on the expedition soon understood that the Hawaiians were related to other Polynesian peoples, and they were initially well received. A year later, they were keen to resume their northern explorations but were forced back with a broken mast, and both ships returned to Hawaii. Misjudging the mood of the Hawaiians, Cook was killed at Kealakekua Bay in February 1779.

Despite its tragic ending, the voyage achieved a great deal. Under Cook's close guidance, artists John Webber and William Ellis created a remarkable visual record. The men of the *Resolution* and *Discovery* extensively documented another important Polynesian society, albeit without fully understanding the nuances of Hawaiian culture. Cook's voyage mapped what it could of north-west America and north-east Asia, from Alaska across the Bering Sea to the Kamchatka peninsula, paving the way for future British trade in the North Pacific.

John Webber (1752–1793)
Indians of Nootka Sound 1778
Petherick Collection (Pictures), National Library of Australia,
Canberra, PIC Drawer 81 #R6879

After leaving Hawaii, the *Resolution* and *Discovery* spent about a
month in Nootka Sound, Vancouver Island. They traded with the
local people and visited their homes. Cook wanted to call them
'Wak'ashians', after the word *wak'ash* which they often used.
Taken in April 1778, Webber's drawing shows the details of a quiver

the Nootka men used for their arrows. Cook noted that their clothes
'are made of the Skins of land and Sea animals, in the making of
which there is very little of either art or trouble'.

William Ellis (1751–1785)
A View in Ship Cove 1778
Pictures Collection, National Library of Australia, Canberra,
PIC Drawer 7418 #R7595

Cook had not overseen preparations for the ships personally and
the *Resolution*'s poor state of repair was a constant problem. This
watercolour scene by Ellis, in a cove at Nootka Sound, shows the
Resolution (at right) partway through the replacement of its foremast.
The rear or mizzenmast was replaced in following days. The ropes
that secured the *Resolution* to pine trees onshore are visible, and the
tents in the foreground belonged to the voyage astronomers.

Wordlist from Nootka Sound (Vancouver Island), North Pacific, f.413r
in James Cook (1728–1779)
Journal 1776–1779
British Library, London, Egerton MS 2177 A
© British Library Board

78.
ril

of homage paid them and we could gain nothing from
information, as we had learnt little more of their
language than to ask the names of things and the
two simple words yes and no. The following list contains most of the words we got of their language; it
will be a sufficient specimen and may in some measure
inable us to find out which of the neighbouring
nations these people bear the most affinity to —
Was I to name them as a Nation I would call them
Wak'ashians, from the word Wak'ash which
they frequently made use of, but rather more with
the Women than the men; it seemed to express, ap-
plause, approbation and friendship; for when they
were satisfied or well pleased with any thing, they
would with one voice call out "Wak'ash wak'ash"!

A

Aï and Aïo	Yes
A'ook or Cheaimis	To eat. To chew.
Ah'koo or Ah'ko	This
A'beesh or Eetche	Displeasure
Alle	I say Friend harkaye.
Asko	Song or large, 'tis as long as this.
Alle or alla	Friend speaking to me, as I say
A'beetszle	To go away, or depart.
At'lieu	The depending pine, or Cypress.
Ah ee uk	A plain bone point for striking (Seals)
Ashee ach sheetle	To yawn.
Aoph	To Whistle.

John Webber (1752–1793)
View of Kealakekua Bay 1779
Pictures Collection, National Library of Australia, Canberra,
PIC Solander Box B16 #PIC/18097

The *Resolution* and *Discovery* spent the rest of 1778 in the very north
of the Pacific, making stops in Prince William Sound in the Gulf
of Alaska and Unalaska in the Aleutian Islands. They returned to
Hawaii in mid-January 1779, anchoring in Kealakekua Bay on the
17th. This view is believed to have been taken on the spot about
a week later, at a time of *kapu* or prohibition. The bay is entirely
devoid of people, unlike on their 1778 visit.

OPPOSITE

Edward Riou (1762–1801)
*A Sketch of Kara'ka'hooah [Kealakekua] Bay in the
Island of Hawhy'hee [Hawaii]*
The National Archives, UK, ADM 352/343
© Crown Copyright – image courtesy of The National Archives

A rare manuscript map of Cook's final days at Kealakekua Bay,
on the Kona coast, Hawaii, Midshipman Riou's sketch shows the
anchorages of the *Resolution* and *Discovery*, and records soundings
taken and the nature of the tides in the bay. Settlements at either
end of the bay include, at the southern end, Hikiau Heiau, a place
of worship where Cook was ritually welcomed. The sheer cliff face
overlooking the bay contained burial caves. Cook was killed near the
village of Ka'awaloa, at the north end of the bay, where observatories
had been stationed. The name of the bay comes from the phrase *ke
ala ke kua*, meaning 'pathway of the god'; it was an area dedicated to
extensive *makahiki* celebrations in honour of the god Lono.

A SKETCH

of

KARA'KA'KOOAH BAY

in the Island

HAWHY'HEE

by Edward Riou

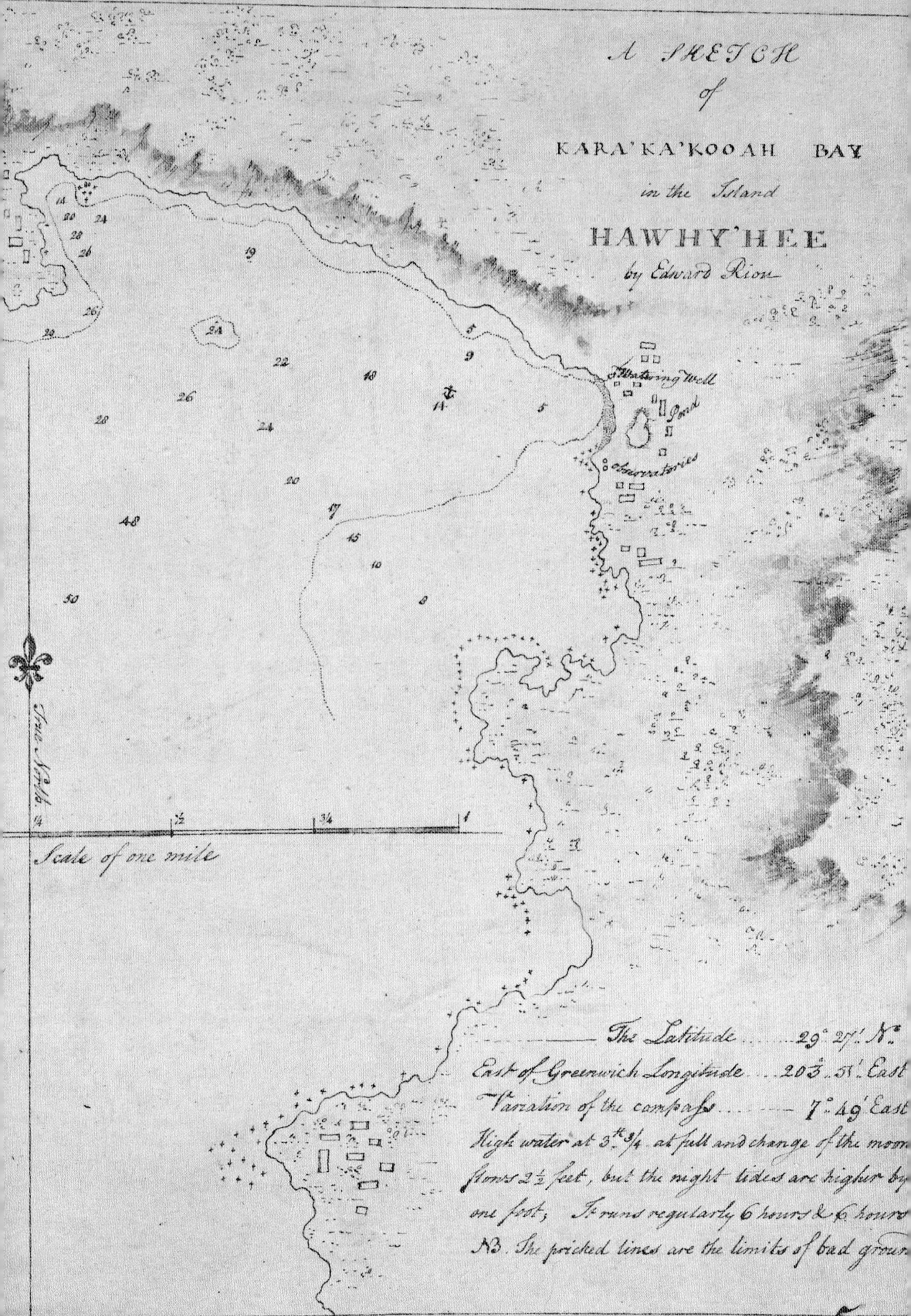

Watering Well

Pond

Observatories

True North

Scale of one mile

The Latitude .... 29° 27' N.

East of Greenwich Longitude ... 203° 5' East

Variation of the compass .... 7° 49' East

High water at 3h ¾ at full and change of the moon

flows 2½ feet, but the night tides are higher by

one feet; It runs regularly 6 hours & 6 hours

N.B. The pricked lines are the limits of bad ground

521

Three Ivory Turtle Ornaments 1778
Australian Museum, Sydney, H000151–001, H000151–002
and H000151–003

Mahiole (Helmet) 1770s
National Gallery of Australia, Canberra, NGA 71.175
Purchased 1971

Spectacular red and yellow feathered helmets and capes were
worn as a mark of distinction by *ali'i* (high-ranking Hawaiians).
They had a basket-weave construction, and their colours came
from the feathers of prized Hawaiian birds, the *i'iwi* (named for its
red feathers) and the *'ō'ō* (yellow feathers). This helmet, believed
to have been collected by Charles Clerke, who sailed with Cook on
all three Pacific voyages, is thought to have been owned by Charles
Francis Greville, a lifelong friend of Sir Joseph Banks.

George Carter (1737–1795)
Death of Captain Cook 1781
Rex Nan Kivell Collection (Pictures), National Library
of Australia, Canberra, PIC Screen 157 #T266

Cook's death at Kealakekua Bay on 14 February 1779 was a moment of high drama and confrontation. In Carter's version, Cook is shown on the attack, using his inverted gun as a club as he confronts the determined Hawaiian chief. However they were depicted, Cook's final moments derived from his attempt to take hostage Kalani'ōpu'u, the *Ali'i nui* (king) of Hawaii Island.

Pahoa (Dagger) of Swordfish Reputed to be the One Which Killed Cook c. 1779
Hooper Collection, Bernice Pauahi Bishop Museum, Honolulu
1977.206.013
Photo by Jesse W. Stephen, copyright © Bishop Museum, 2018;
Bishop Museum Archives

The Cook journals describe many situations in which Pacific islander peoples and Europeans miscommunicated, but few led to the sort of violence seen at Kealakekua Bay. The return of Cook following *makahiki* (the season that honours the god Lono), compounded misperceptions about property, theft and exchange of gifts. Cook's reactions to the thefts, or what were to *kanaka maoli* (native Hawaiians) merely the use and enjoyment of things, led to a chain of events that culminated in his death.

Though eyewitness accounts record that Cook was killed by an iron dagger, stories have persisted that a swordfish-bill dagger was used. This dagger was collected by naturalist Andrew Bloxam of HMS *Blonde* in 1825, who noted, 'Probably the dagger used in the death of Capt. Cook'. The *Blonde* visited the morai (sacred meeting place and burial ground) at Kealakekua Bay, and collected a number of relics. Naval officer George Anson Byron had led the voyage to Hawaii to return the bodies of King Kamehameha II and Queen Kamāmalu, who had died of measles in July 1824 while on a visit to England.

James Cook (1728–1779)
Fragment of the Logbook of Cook, Third Pacific Voyage (detail)
28 November 1778 – 17 January 1779
British Library, London, Egerton MS 2177 B, f.3r
© British Library Board

Cook's voyage journal breaks off on 6 January 1779, at which point
the *Resolution* had just passed south of the main island of Hawaii.

This fragment of his log (used to record operational matters) is folio
size, and contains the last entries Cook wrote. The entries for long
days at sea are compressed into a line or two of narrative, leaving the
recording of details to his officers. The log ends on 17 January 1779,
when the ships anchored at Kealakekua Bay.

TOP

Entry for 14 February 1779
in Charles Clerke (1741–1779)
Log 14 February – 26 July 1779
The National Archives, UK, ADM 55/124, f.3r
© Crown Copyright – image courtesy of The National Archives

After Cook's death Charles Clerke, *Discovery*'s captain, assumed command of the expedition. He witnessed the event from aboard ship and later wrote to the Admiralty that there were no reprisals and that Cook's remains were returned. Other observers later stated that Clerke had quickly taken steps to prevent further outbursts of violence, which meant the expedition could resume. However, according to expedition surgeon David Samwell, Clerke was prevailed upon to fire cannon on a crowd on the shore. Next day, a shore party burnt down some houses, shot several men and beheaded two others. The Hawaiians responded with contempt, exposing their buttocks or hurling stones and spears. Eventually a sort of peace was agreed and, eight days after Cook's death, *Resolution* and *Discovery* left Kealakekua Bay.

BOTTOM

Attributed to William Harvey (1752–1807)
Account of the Death of James Cook c. 1779
Manuscripts Collection, National Library of Australia, Canberra, MS 8

At the end of a voyage all the logs and journals kept by men in the pay of the navy had to be submitted to the Admiralty. This was required not only for security reasons, but also because the Admiralty wanted nothing to steal the thunder of the voyage's official account. This account of Cook's death, which recent research suggests was written by William Harvey, midshipman on the voyage, does not appear to have been published.

William Wade Ellis (1751–1785)
View in Avacha Bay, Kamchatka 1779
Rex Nan Kivell Collection (Pictures), National Library
of Australia, Canberra, PIC Solander Box B7 #T211 NK53/1

After Cook's death, the ships made their way north-west to the
Russian outpost of Kamchatka. After years at sea, with no contact
with Europeans, they met with Major Magnus Carl von Behm, the
German commandant of Kamchatka at that time. Von Behm received
the expedition warmly and helped them with supplies. Charles
Clerke had become commander of the expedition, but he was
suffering from tuberculosis and died at Kamchatka in August 1779.

William Wade Ellis (1751–1785)
Winter View of Kamtschatska May 1779
Rex Nan Kivell Collection (Pictures), National Library
of Australia, Canberra, PIC Solander Box A41 #T208 NK53/F

In his memoirs, Ellis recorded how 'on the 12th a party was
sent to cut wood, and our empty casks were got on shore to repair'.
In the distance is the town and harbour of St Peter and St Paul.

Winter View of Kamtschatska

John Webber (1752–1793)
A Woman of Kamschatka 1779
Rex Nan Kivell Collection (Pictures), National Library
of Australia, Canberra, PIC Drawer 84 #T429 NK52/F

The Indigenous people of Kamchatka had adopted Russian
fashions. James King noted that 'the Married women had
hansome Silk Handkerchiefs bound round their heads'.

John Webber (1752–1793)
A Man of Kamschatka 1779
Rex Nan Kivell Collection (Pictures), National Library
of Australia, Canberra, PIC Drawer 84 #T428 NK52/E

John Webber (1752–1793)
A Woman of Kamschatka 1779
Rex Nan Kivell Collection (Pictures), National Library
of Australia, Canberra, PIC Drawer 84 #T429 NK52/F

John Webber (1752–1793)
A Man of Kamschatka 1779
Rex Nan Kivell Collection (Pictures), National Library
of Australia, Canberra, PIC Drawer 84 #T428 NK52/E

John Webber (1752–1793)
Kamchatka Winter Habitation 1780s
Rex Nan Kivell Collection (Pictures), National Library
of Australia, Canberra, PIC Drawer 84 #T431 NK52/H

The homes of the Indigenous people of Kamchatka fascinated the
Europeans. Russian fur traders were well established there and the
surgeon David Samwell noted that since the Russians had arrived in
the area the previous habit of building yurts with doors on the top
had given way to a new form of construction in which they were
now placed on the side.

John Webber (1752–1793)
Manner of Travelling in Kamtschatka 1779
Rex Nan Kivell Collection (Pictures), National Library
of Australia, Canberra, PIC Drawer 84 #T426 NK52/C

It is thought that this work depicts a scene witnessed by John Gore,
James King and the artist in May 1779. In the official account, King
described what were typically one-person sleds:

> *The dogs are usually five in number, yoked, two and two with a leader.
> The reins not being fastened to the head of the dogs, but to the collar,
> have little power over them, and are generally hung upon the sledge,
> whilst the driver depends entirely on their obedience to his voice for the
> direction of them … The driver is also provided with a crooked stick,
> which answers the purpose both of whip and reins; as by striking it into
> the snow, he is enabled to moderate the speed of the dogs, or even to
> stop them entirely.*

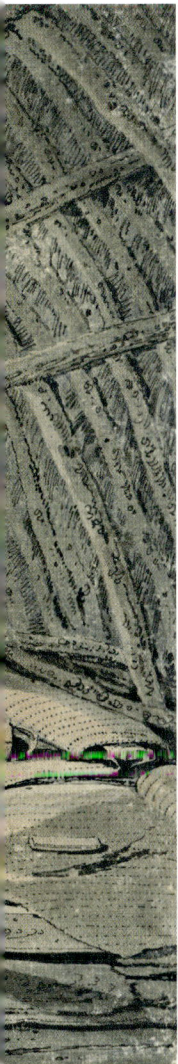

131

7. COLLECTING COOK

Cook's death attracted huge attention in Britain and across Europe. Catherine the Great of Russia was 'greatly concern'd' to hear of his 'untimely death', as was George III of England. An unfinished tapa (barkcloth) coat embroidered by Cook's wife, Elizabeth, suggests her own reaction to the news. Cook's exploits were written up and memorialised in different ways, in print, image and object. There were also various performances, the most notable of which was perhaps the blockbuster pantomime production *Omai, or, a Trip Round the World* designed by Strasbourg-born artist Philippe Jacques de Loutherbourg which opened in Covent Garden in December 1785. The play concluded with a painted backdrop showing Cook being carried heavenward.

Meanwhile, accounts by the officers, crew, scientists and artists who had sailed with Cook proliferated. Official accounts and maps had to be finalised, and the extensive collections of objects consolidated, just as had occurred in the 1770s, after Cook's two earlier Pacific voyages.

To the PUBLIC. The Death of Captain JAMES COOK.

THIS great Navigator, who braved every danger, and whose genius seemed calculated for difficult researches, had discovered a knot of islands, lying in north latitude 21 deg. 28 min. east longitude 203 deg. 25 min. which, in compliment to his patron, the then First Lord of the Admiralty, he called the Sandwich Islands. One of them was named O-wye-hee ; and from the accounts the author collected from the gentlemen, who, during a long study, did him the favour to live and commune with him, produced every thing that could delight mankind :—They found here a commodious and pleasing bay, safe moorings, and a very hospitable friendly people. On their arrival, curiosity at seeing such wonderful machines, in comparison with theirs, had drawn together near 600 canoes, with people who gave them a very cordial reception : Here they staid near three weeks, during which time they lived in uninterrupted habits of intimacy and esteem. The little barter went on with things most rare to each other—they received from us a variety of little trinkets, beads, &c. but the things they appeared most fond of, were hatchets, knives, nails, and any thing forged in the shape of any of their pahooes, which were of hard wood, were highly acceptable. Our great countryman knew the short way to the human heart; he knew (like his science) how to conciliate the tempers and dispositions of men, whatever were their colour or complexion :—He ordered to be forged pahooes for their Chiefs, and received from them in return cloaks, somewhat of the toga form ; they were netted with delicate fine packthread, and so interwoven with short and long red, brown, black and bright yellow feathers, with casques, so elegantly formed to match them, and so well calculated to resist any intended injury from any weapons they knew of, that the most refined ages of Greece or Rome would not have gone beyond them, and, when habited in them, could not fail of commanding attention ; for nothing could appear more noble or more martial,—Visits on board, and the treat returned on shore by the natives, made the time pass lightly ; the sailors forgot their past perils, and all was joy. It will not be wondered at, that when the time came to depart, to explore perilous icy latitudes, almost every heart was sad, at least those whose only business was to live from day to day ;—they were accompanied out of the Bay with every token of departing friends, and by some, as I have been credibly informed, with infinite regret, wishing and desiring to be left behind. They had sailed four days, in hard blowing weather, (all hands employed in pumping and baling) in examining these islands, when they found their fore-mast sprung in two places, and which absolutely demanded reparation, or a new one, before they venture farther ; and as they might not probably find so convenient an harbour, or such friends or assistance to adjust the matter, it was judged necessary to return to Karrakacooah Bay, which they [reach]ed the seventh day.

[Their] return filled the Indians with surprise, and some began to suspect the sincerity of their new [prof]essors were erected, and the top-mast struck with all expedition ; and Mr. Clevely and his [men] on shore, repairing or making new cleets to it. At the dawn of the morning they observed [a] boat a-stern had been stolen, supposed for the iron that was about it. Capt. Cook desired [a boa]t to go on shore, and endeavour to recover it, or bring off the Chiefs. Clarke was in [a plac]e, and begged of the Commodore to excuse him on the account of his health, being so [in a gr]eat flurry would undo him. The unfortunate Cook took the command himself, and [ordered] boats to be manned and armed, and stationed in different parts of the Bay, to prevent [them] escaping. Mr. Bligh, the master, was sent in the large cutter to intercept a large [canoe] was fired at from the ship, and chaced by the cutter, but escaped by running into

[...] of the mates, with four midshipmen, viz. Messrs. Charlton, Gilbert, Trevanion [and] the small cutter, was ordered to lay off the North Point ; Captain Cook, with [and?] nine marines, went in the pinnace to the North Town, where they landed.

Lieutenant Williams was stationed in the launch off the North Town. When the Captain had landed, he went into the town and enquired for Terriaboo ; he saw his two sons, who presently conducted them to his hut. Lieutenant Philips went in and found the Chief just waking ; the Captain invited them to go a-board the ship, which they readily agreed to, and they went toward the waterside for that purpose, where they were stopped by a woman crying, whose husband was killed the preceding day in an affray, and two chiefs, who obliged Terriaboo to sit down. During this time the natives were arming ; and while the woman was telling her tale to her king, a priest drew off the attention of Captain Cook, by singing a sort of hymn to him.—The Indians now came down in great numbers, and threw an incredible number of stones with their hands and slings.—The marines, with Lieutenant Philips, being formed upon a piece of rock, near to the water's-edge.—The Captain ordered them to fire ; a volley was given, and he called out to them to take to their boats. Lieut. Philips was knocked down by one of the Indians, but recovering, while the fellow was aiming another blow at him, Mr. Philips shot him dead, which caused them for a moment to fall back, and in that moment Capt. Philips saved himself by swimming to the boat. The Captain was dressed in a white jacket and trowsers, and had a double-barrel gun ; he had discharged both, and had turned the butt end of it, and was defending himself and retreating to the pinnace, which he had just reached, when he received a stab in the shoulder by a Chief, and with an iron tuck, made him a present of a few days before by the Captain. The force of the blow, and his being near the edge of the water, he struggled, and at last fell. They gave a savage shout, rushed into the water after him, and, taking him by the hair of his head, plunged their daggers into his neck and breast till he was dead. Mr. Roberts, whose portrait as an officer in the pinnace may be seen, ordered the boat to push off, taking in at the same time some wounded marines, who had fled from the rock.

During this melancholy rencounter, Mr. Gore, commanding officer of the Resolution, fired great guns upon the town ; and Mr. Lanyon, and the young gentlemen in the jolly-boat, defended, to the utmost in their power, their Captain ; and it was with difficulty they could be persuaded to leave their perilous situation. Many of the Indians were killed. Our loss was four marines killed, and several wounded. One of them was wounded with a wooden spear, which struck him just between the eyes, and broke in his head :—The poor fellow suffered excruciating pain for six weeks, when one day holding his head over his hammock, the piece came out of itself, and measured above an inch long ; the man got well, but lost one of his eyes.

No tongue can express the consternation on board, when the boats returned with the loss of this great character ; a loss, in which not England only, but the whole universe, seemed interested—Her Imperial Majesty of all the Russias paid him every attention, and caused his dispatches from Kamschatka, to be conveyed over her immense territory safely to England.—And, to the eternal glory of the French Court, they also, in the midst of war, ordered all cruisers, of whatever class or order, bearing their flag, to respect these sons of peril, and not only to suffer them to pass unmolested, but to shew them every attention, and to succour them, to the utmost of their power, should they fall in their way.

Columbus, Vasco de Gama, Americo Vespucci, Magellan, Davis, Van Dieman, Drake, Raleigh, Dampier and Berens ; Lord Anson, Byron and Bougainville, Wallis and Lord Mulgrave had transcendent merit as navigators, went through innumerable difficulties, and explored much !—But Cook reduced navigation and the preservation of his men to a certainty, and three times circumnavigated the world !—when, returning to his native home, that longed to enfold him, after fruitlessly attempting to find the north-west and north-east passages, and a voyage of four years, he met this unhappy catastrophe ; and where is the breast that does not heave a sigh at the misfortune ?

Entered at the Stationers Hall.

Windsor Castle Jan. 11. 1780.
m 59 pt. 9 P.M.

It is impossible for any One who interests himself in the prosecution
of Nautical Discoverys not to regret the loss of so able and
honest Man as Captain Cooke; I should imagine that Capt.
Clarke though a good Sailor from the roughness of his sentiments
is not calculated to go through his coverys with that Temper
which seemed so remarkably to attend his worthy predecessor

James Harris, 1st Earl of Malmesbury (1746–1820)
Letter to Lord Sandwich 18 January 1780
Manuscripts Collection, National Library of Australia, Canberra,
MS 7218, Item 40

News of Cook's death filtered through to the Russian court in
St Petersburg from the outpost at Kamchatka in Siberia, which
the British voyagers, now under the command of Charles Clerke,
visited after Cook's death. Sir James Harris, envoy extraordinary
to Catherine the Great, reported back to Lord Sandwich that 'the
Empress … was greatly concern'd at the untimely death of Capt
Cooke, & was exceedingly anxious to know whether it had
happen'd in any of the Islands under her protection or making
part of her dominions'.

FOLLOWING PAGE

Elizabeth Cook (1742–1835)
Letter to Lord Sandwich, First Lord of the Admiralty 13 June 1781
Sandwich Papers, Captain Cook Memorial Museum, Whitby,
WHICC.174.545
© CCMM Whitby

Cook's widow, Elizabeth, wrote from Mile End, asking the First
Lord of the Admiralty 'to consider us for such compensation as
you may deem us deserving' and seeking 'your Lordships favour
and protection'. She notes how she and her family 'became great
sufferers from his not returning safe home'.

My Lord,   Petersburgh – Jan:y 4 1780
                                                        18

I was preparing to send to your Lordship
every information I could collect relative to the Ships
which had appear'd in the neighbourhood of the
Aleutonian Islands, when the Express came from
the Commandant of Kamtschatka & the letters
bringing the melancholy account of the Death of
Capt Cooke came to my hands: This Event flung
a damp on my enquirys, which were indeed become
useless, from the facts being now compleatly ascertain'd,
& the accurate Relation of the expedition thus far
naturaly set forth in Capt Clerkes packet to Mr
Stephens.

Besides the Empress Herself, whose active
mind attends to every pursuit which may concern the

Earl of Sandwich   good

OPPOSITE

Waistcoat of Tahiti Cloth (Tapa) for Captain Cook to Wear at Court, Had He Returned from His Third Voyage, Embroidered by Mrs Elizabeth Cook c. 1779
State Library of New South Wales, Sydney, R 198

The unfinished waistcoat is one of the great surviving cross-cultural objects associated with Cook. He is believed to have acquired the tapa (barkcloth) in the Society Islands, on his second Pacific voyage, and brought it home to England. Elizabeth began embroidering it for him to wear at court, but never completed it. By the time it was exhibited at the Colonial and Indian Exhibition in London in 1886

in 'a collection of relics' of Cook, it was in the possession of one of her relatives, the Reverend Frederick Bennett, Vicar of Maddington. It was subsequently purchased by the New South Wales colonial government.

Cook mentions receiving tapa at various times in his journal. For example, on Saturday 11 September 1773, he exchanged items with Oreo, of Bora Bora (Society Islands): 'Early in the Morn I had a Viset from Oreo and his Son, a youth about 12 or 13 years of age, the latter brought me a Hog, a piece of Cloth and some fruit for which I gave him an Ax, dress'd him out in a Shirt and other things which made him not a little proud of him self.'

Late Victorian Copy of Captain Cook's 1789 Coat of Arms
c. 31 August 1892
Pictures Collection, National Library of Australia, Canberra,
PIC Drawer 12871 #PIC/9025

Elizabeth Cook petitioned for a coat of arms, and it was granted
in 1789; it was to be borne by his descendants and placed on any
monument to his memory. It incorporates a globe centred on the
Pacific Ocean, with an eight-pointed star at each pole. Elizabeth
also received the 'Letters Patent', a vellum document with wax seals
now held by the State Library of New South Wales. This is a copy
of the official register of the College of Arms, London, presumably
following an enquiry by someone interested in Cook.

Wedgwood and Bentley (1768–80)
Portrait Medallion of Captain Cook c. 1777
Pictures Collection, National Library of Australia, Canberra,
PIC Object Drawer 3 #PIC/12018

An early Wedgwood work, this medallion is based on James Basire's
widely circulated engraving, which was itself based on William
Hodges' portrait of Cook.

Thomas R. Poole (1765–1837)
Wax Portrait Relief of Captain James Cook 1795–1815
Pictures Collection, National Library of Australia, Canberra,
PIC Object Drawer 19 #PIC/14683

A label on the reverse of this work suggests that this keepsake was
presented by the artist to the Princess of Wales, Princess Caroline of
Brunswick. Poole, who specialised in wax portraits, has modelled
this relief after Nathaniel Dance's oil portrait.

Lewis Pingo (1743–1830)
Commemorative Medal to Celebrate the Voyages of Captain James Cook 1784
Pictures Collection, National Library of Australia, Canberra, PIC Row 62/6/4 #A4000451l/19

In 1784 the Royal Society, London's premier scientific body, released a medal to honour Cook's memory. He had been elected a fellow in 1776, after the second Pacific voyage. Available in gold, silver and bronze, it was funded by subscribers. The Latin inscription around the medal's edge acknowledges 'James Cook, the most intrepid investigator of the seas'. On the reverse is a tag adapted from Horace, *Nil intentatum nostri liquere* ('No path to fame left untried').

Wedgwood
Portrait Medallion of Joseph Banks c. 1785
Pictures Collection, National Library of Australia, Canberra, PIC Object Drawer 3 #PIC/14641

The *Endeavour* voyage of 1768–71 gave Joseph Banks an expertise on all things Pacific and exposure as a man of science. This medallion, designed for Wedgwood by the sculptor and draughtsman John Flaxman, reflects Banks' growing reputation after the *Endeavour* voyage. He was elected President of the Royal Society in 1778, a position he held until his death in 1820.

Joshua Reynolds (1723–1792)
Omai of the Friendly Isles c. 1774
Rex Nan Kivell Collection (Pictures), National Library
of Australia, PIC Drawer 7811 #PIC2711 NK9670

The *Adventure*, captained by Tobias Furneaux, returned to England
in 1774, carrying the Ra'iatean man Omai (more properly, Mai).
Mai spent about two years being fêted in society in London, living
at the expense of Joseph Banks. He met King George III and Banks'
friend from the *Endeavour* voyage, Daniel Solander; he also met the
novelist Fanny Burney, whose brother James had been an officer in
the *Adventure*. This is a study for Joshua Reynolds' major portrait in
oil, and was likely taken from life. Reynolds was the leading society
portraitist of the day, and first President of the Royal Academy of
Arts (1768–92).

Omai of the Friendly Isles

Presents for Omai 1776
Papers of Sir Joseph Banks (Manuscripts)
National Library of Australia, Canberra, MS 9 Item 13

Presents for Omai

4 Suits of Cloths of Light materials with
a proper apartment of suitables .
a few shoes & stockings extra

16 Toys models houses of Coaches waggons Sedan chairs &c.

3 Apartment of Iron

1 do. of linnens

16. do. of Beads

12 a feild bed.

4 2 Whip saws

10 a table - to be made on board

11 a chair do.

13 a chest of drawers

14 a wheelbarrow to be made on board

5 — Planes

6 — Files

2 4 Suits of Womens cloths compleat.

7 a Case of Knives & Forks

8 12 pewter plates

8— 9 Sauce pans & kettles for boiling

9 mugs a glasses & Spoons

9—10 flints & steels for striking fire

15 2 drums

142

Playbill for 'Omai, or a Trip Round the World', Monday 26 December 1785
Australian Printed Collection,
National Library of Australia, Canberra, PA Broadside 103

The pantomime was first performed at Covent Garden Theatre in December 1785. It was produced at a time of peak interest in the Pacific voyages, a year after Cook's third voyage account was published. It was, as one contemporary commentator put it, 'the stage edition of Captain Cook's voyage'.

At the Theatre Royal, Covent Garden,

This present MONDAY, December 26, 1785,
Will be presented the TRAGEDY of

GEORGE BARNWELL.

Barnwell by Mr. FARREN,
And Millwood by Mrs. BATES.

To which will be added, for the FIFTH Time, a NEW PANTOMIME, called

OMAI:

Or, A Trip Round the World.

TOWHA, the Guardian Genius of OMAI's Anceſtors, by Mrs. RIVERS,
OTOO, Father of OMAI, by Mr. DARLEY, OMAI by Mr. BLURTON,
HARLEQUIN, Servant to OMAI, by Mr. KENNEDY,
OEDIDDEE, Pretender to the Throne, by Mrs. KENNEDY,
OBEREA, an Enchantreſs, by Mrs. MARTYR, BRITANNIA by Mrs. INCHBALD,
Don STRUTTOLANDO, Rival to OMAI, by Mr. PALMER,
CLOWN, his Servant, and Rival to HARLEQUIN, by Mr. D'ELPINI,
Father of LONDINA by Mr. THOMPSON,
Mother by Mrs. DAVENETT,
LONDINA, the Conſort deſtined to OMAI, by Miſs CRANFIELD,
COLOMBINE, Maid to LONDINA, by Miſs ROWSON,
Old FAIRY, Friend to HARLEQUIN, by Mr. WEWITZER,
Engliſh Captain by Mr. BRETT, Juſtice by Mr. DAVIES,
And A Travelled OTAHEITEAN, with SONGS, by Mr. EDWIN.

With a PROCESSION

Of the Inhabitants of Otaheite, New Zealand, Tanna, Marqueſas, the Friendly, Sandwich, and Eaſter Iſlands; Tſchutzki, Siberia, Kamtſchatka, Nootka Sound, Onalaſhka, Prince William's Sound, and the other Countries viſited by Captain COOK, exactly repreſenting their Dreſſes, and Weapons.

The Pantomime, and the whole of the Scenery, Machinery, Dreſſes, &c.

Deſigned and Invented by Mr. LOUTHERBOURG,

And Executed under his Superintendance and Direction by

Meſſrs. RICHARDS, CARVER, and HODGINGS,
Mr. CATTON, jun. Mr. TURNER,
AND A CELEBRATED ARTIST.

The Muſic entirely New, compoſed by Mr. SHIELD.

⁂ BOOKS containing a ſhort Account of the Pantomime, as well as the Recitatives, Airs, Duets, Trios, and Choruſſes, and a Deſcription of the Proceſſion, to be had at the Theatre.

Nothing under FULL PRICE will be taken.

To-morrow, the Comedy of SHE STOOPS to CONQUER.

Philippe Jacques de Loutherbourg (1740–1812)
Toha, Chief of Otahaite 1785
Pictures Collection, National Library of Australia, Canberra,
PIC Solander Box A68 #R142

The National Library of Australia holds 18 original costume designs
for the pantomime *Omai*, each representing figures from across the
Pacific, brought together in praise of Omai. Although much of its
material was whimsical and inaccurate, *Omai* helped shape views
of the Pacific Ocean and its inhabitants. The costume designs have
been annotated by voyage artist John Webber, and came to the
Library in volumes of proof engravings that had passed through
his hands. The whereabouts of the design for Omai's costume is
unknown. When de Loutherbourg's effects were sold in June 1812,
they were found to include Society Islands costumes which one
historian has claimed were 'no doubt used … in staging *Omai*'.
This is one of two designs for a figure wearing a Tahitian chief's
characteristic breast ornament, or *tāumi*.

OPPOSITE

Attributed to Philippe Jacques de Loutherbourg (1740–1812) after
John Webber (1752–1793)
Drums Otaheite. Idols Sandwich Isles. Paddles. Altar c. 1785
Alexander Turnbull Library, Wellington, B-091-009

De Loutherbourg collaborated with voyage artist John Webber, who
provided source material for the costume designs and scenes.

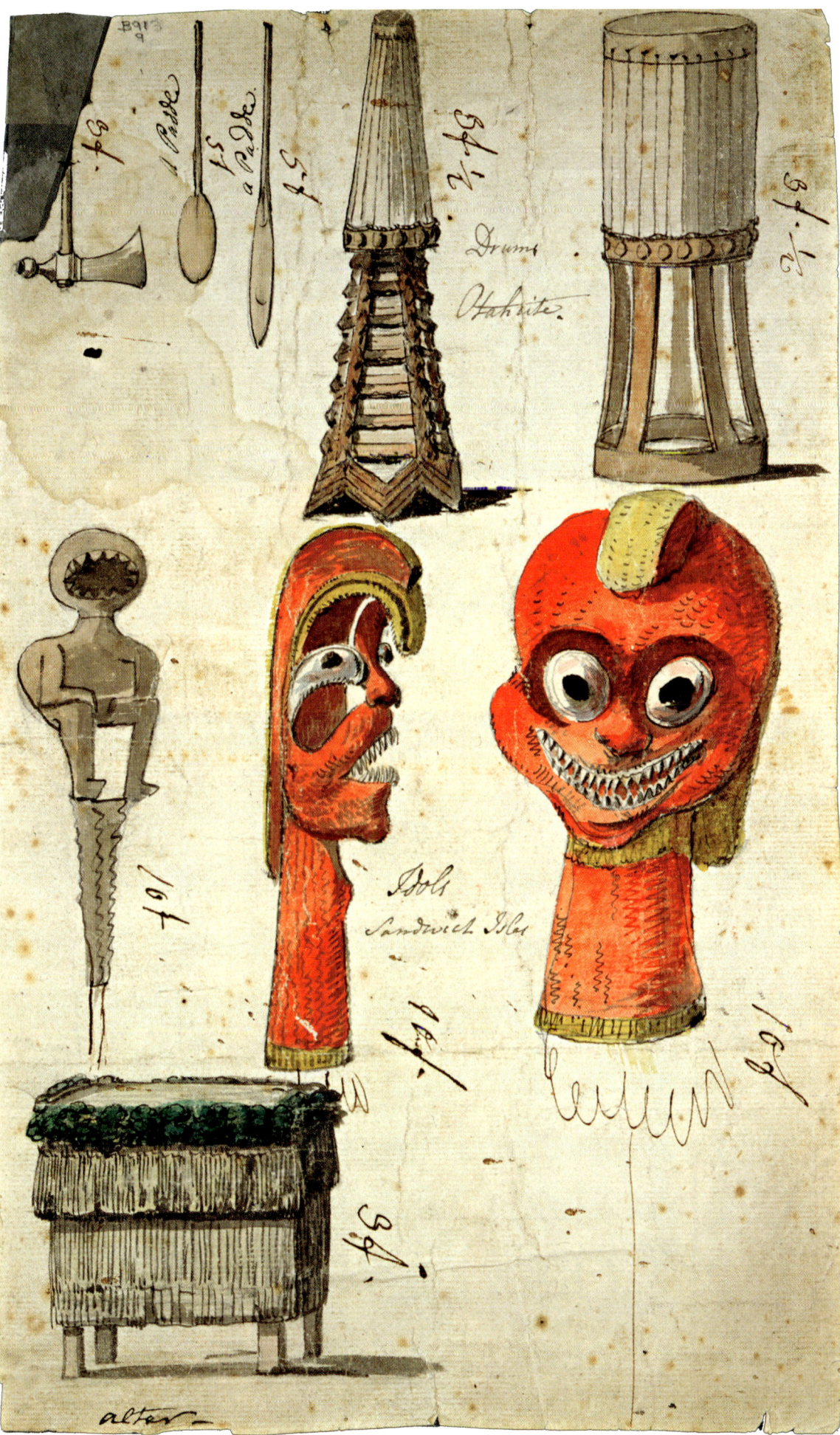

B913
9

1 Paddle

a Paddle

2 fig

Drums

Otaheite

fig. 1/2

Idols

Sandwich Isles

alter

John Elliott (1759–1834)
'The Names of the Officers and Civilians on the Quarter deck of the Resolution', in *Memoirs of the Early Life of John Elliott, of Elliott House, Esq. and Lieut. of the Royal Navy* early 19th century
British Library, London, Add MS 42714, f.1v
© British Library Board

Elliott was only about 13 when he sailed with Cook on his second Pacific voyage. Many years later, he wrote his memoirs, 'at the request of his Wife, for the use and amusement of his Children <u>only</u>'. In themselves, they are not particularly unusual. The list that prefaces them, however, is quite special. In it Elliott provides a character assessment of men on the *Resolution*.

(He also guesses their ages, though somewhat inaccurately.) Cook is 'Sober—Brave, Humane and exelent Seaman and Officer'; Charles Clerke is 'A brave and good officer, & a genal favourite'; Richard Pickersgill is 'A good officer and astronomer, but liking ye Grog'; naturalist Johann Reinhold Forster is 'A clever but a litigious quarelsom, fellow'; voyage artist William Hodges is a 'Clever good man'; midshipman Thomas Willis is 'wild and drinking'; and midshipman George Vancouver is 'a Quiet inoffensive Young man'.

John Elliott (1759–1834)
Captain Cook's Vessel the Resolution in the South Pacific 1774
Pictures Collection, National Library of Australia, Canberra,
PIC Drawer 7419 #R9038

Many of the men who sailed on Cook's voyages kept the things
they made or collected. On the reverse of this painting, one of two
works by Elliott in the Library's collection, is an inscription reading,
'This belongs to Mrs Elliott'. The Library also possesses a piece of
corduroy 'made from the bark of native trees to replace clothing on
Capt. Cook's second voyage', and a scrap from Cook's draft of his
second Pacific voyage journal, written in his own hand.

A Companion to the Museum (Late Sir Ashton Lever's) 1790
Petherick Collection (Australian Printed), National Library
of Australia, Canberra, FRM F88a

Sir Ashton Lever's museum was the repository of many things
collected on Cook voyages. It had opened in 1775 in Leicester
Square in central London and was known as the Holophusicon
(from two Greek words meaning 'whole' and 'natural'), or more
commonly as the Leverian Museum. Sir Ashton commissioned
the artist Sarah Stone to record the contents of the museum over
a number of years. This companion was published soon after the
museum moved to new premises in Albion Street, two years after
its founder's death in 1788. The frontispiece is based on Stone's
own rendering of the museum's interior. Many objects collected on
Cook's Pacific voyages were displayed in what this catalogue calls
'the Sandwich Room'. The museum's contents were dispersed in a
sale in 1806.

John Montagu, 4th Earl of Sandwich (1718–1792)
Autograph Letter to Sir Joseph Banks from Hinchingbrooke
19 August 1775
The Mulgrave Archives, Lent by the Marquis of Normanby,
WHICC.110

In this lively letter to Banks, Lord Sandwich refers to the *Endeavour*'s
naturalist, Daniel Solander, and to his own mistress, Martha Ray:

> *I delivered a live Cameleon to Dr Solander, it was in perfect health
> & spirits, so that if you do not receive it safe & sound it is no fault of
> mine. One of Miss Ray's new paroqueets died of a fit, I had a great
> battle with her whither the corps should go to you or to Mr Lever,
> I was against you but, she carried her point, as women generally do
> when they are in earnest.*

It is likely that both the chameleon and the parakeet were collected
on Cook's second Pacific voyage. Ray was murdered by an infatuated
clergyman in 1779.

Daines Barrington (1727/8–1800)
Letter to Lord Sandwich 3 October 1780
Papers of Lord Sandwich (Manuscripts), National Library
of Australia, Canberra, MS 7218, Item 5

Barrington was a lawyer and naturalist. His letter reveals the role
Lord Sandwich played as a broker for Cook voyage items:

> *As I conceive that the Discovery ships are by this time in the river
> may I take the liberty of reminding your Lordship of Sr Ashton
> Lever's pretensions to those specimens which were collected by the
> Capts Cooke & Clarke. I know well that my friend Sr Ashton thinks
> himself so much already oblig'd to your Lordships for some valuable
> additions to his Museum that he would be sorry these his pretensions
> should be mention'd … did he not suppose this his claim may deserve
> consideration in case any previous applications had been made to your
> Lordship by others.*

My Lord.   Beckett Octobr: 3.
                                                        1780

as I conceive that
the Discovery ships are by this
time in the river may I take
the liberty of reminding your
Lordship of Sr Ashton Lever's pre-
-tensions to those specimens which
were collected by the Capts Cooke &
Clarke.

          I know well that my
friend Sr Ashton thinks himself
so much already oblig'd to your
Lordships for some valuable addi-
-tions to his Museum that he
would be sorry these his pretensions
should be mention'd according to

Johann Reinhold Forster (1729–1798)
An Account of a Voyage Round the World in the Years 1772–1775
Sandwich Papers, Captain Cook Memorial Museum, Whitby,
WHICC.174.36.29A
© CCMM Whitby

After Cook's second Pacific voyage, there followed a remarkably
acrimonious exchange between the Earl of Sandwich and Johann
Reinhold Forster. The Forsters had carried out their observations
diligently. On his return to London, the elder Forster argued that
the Admiralty had agreed that he should write the account of the
voyage, sharing the profits with Cook—claims the Admiralty denied.
As the work developed, Forster resisted having his manuscript
edited, and stated that he intended to publish it in French.

Lord Sandwich reminded him of his debt to the Crown, and made
clear that if he pursued this plan, 'all concert with me must be at
an end'. Having examined the manuscript, he added pointedly,
'whether your narrative is written in French or in English, I think
it does not make the minutest degree of difference'. Forbidden to
publish anything until the official Cook volumes appeared, Forster
circumvented the order by arranging for his son Georg to write
A Voyage Round the World in His Britannic Majesty's Sloop Resolution
(1777) from his own journals. In 1778 Forster published his own
Observations Made During a Voyage Round the World, a work of
considerable scientific merit.

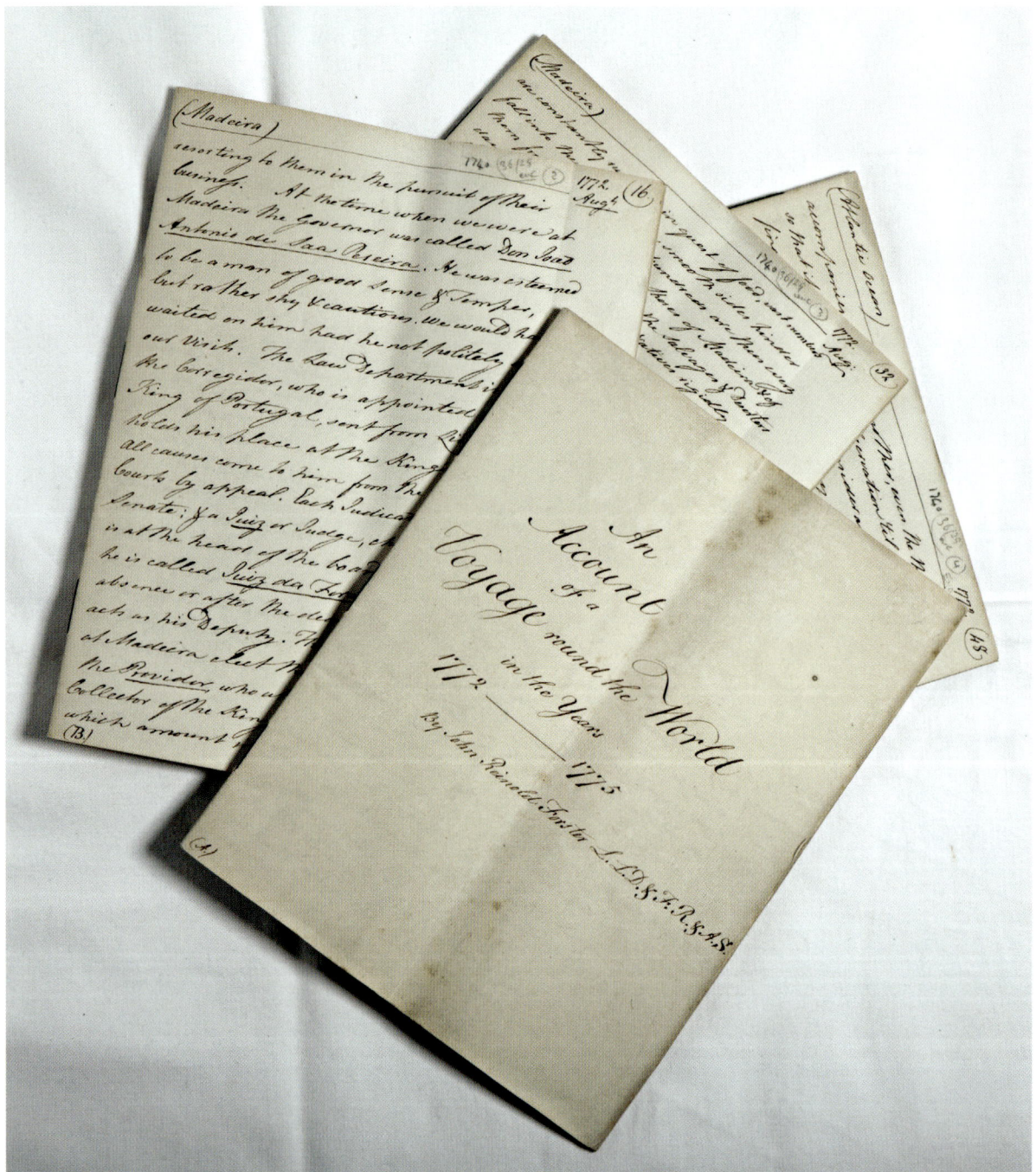

Jean François Rigaud (1742–1810)
Portrait of Dr Johann Reinhold Forster
and His Son Georg Forster c. 1780
National Portrait Gallery, Canberra, Accession number 2009.55
Purchased with funds provided by the Liangis family,
the Ian Potter Foundation and John Schaeffer AO 2009

This famous double portrait of the Forsters—both of whom sailed with Cook on the second Pacific voyage, Johann as scientist and Georg as scientific draughtsman—shows the pair at work together in New Zealand. They had secured their positions on the voyage through the assistance of Daines Barrington after Joseph Banks withdrew. Georg, an accomplished artist, is sketching while his father holds a bellbird; in his hatband is a botanical specimen (*Forstera sedifolia*) named after them. The painting was exhibited at London's Royal Academy in 1781, though with the inaccurate title 'Portrait of Dr Forster and his son on the Island of Otaheite'.

Catalogue of Drawings and of Portraits in Oyl by Mr. Webber.

Island of Desolation or Kerguelans Land   No. 1

1	A distant view of Christmas Harbour	}	In the Roll
2	A View of Christmas Harbour		
3	A Plant of Ditto		

New Holland. Van Deemans Land No. 2

4	A Portrait of a Woman	}	In the Porte feuille
5	A Ditto of a Man		
6	An Animal called the Opossum		
7	The S.E. part of Adventure Bay	}	Roll
8	An Interview between Captr. Cook, & the Natives		

New Zealand   No. 3.

9	A Portrait of a Chief	}	Porte feuille
10	A distant view of a Hippah		
11	The Hippah		
12	A General view of Queen Charlottes Sound	}	Roll
13	A representation of the Natives in their temporary habitations		

The Friendly Islands. No. 4

| 14 | A Boxing Match | } | Porte feuille |
| 15 | King Pawlehow drinking his Cava, and attended by the Principal Chiefs of the Island | | |

Unknown scribe, after John Webber (1752–1793)
Catalogue of Drawings and of Portraits in Oyl by Mr Webber, Annotated by Joseph Banks 1780s
Papers of Sir Joseph Banks (Manuscripts), National Library of Australia, Canberra, MS 9 Item 140

One of the most remarkable manuscripts in the National Library of Australia's collection, this is the best surviving list of Webber's voyage-related works of art. It was no doubt completed for Banks, who has annotated it in pencil. Banks played a key role in the management of the publication of the official account of Cook's third Pacific voyage. This list is invaluable for determining the extent of Webber's artistic output.

French Paper for the Plates to the Voyage c. 1782–83
Papers of Sir Joseph Banks (Manuscripts), National Library of Australia, Canberra, MS 9 Item 16

Bookseller and publisher George Nicol was the publisher of the 1784 account of Cook's third Pacific voyage. This list from Banks' papers suggests the logistical complexity of the publication.

French Paper for the plates to the Voyage

There are about 30 of the plates that will require 1/2 Sheets And there are about 35 of them that may be printed on 1/4 Sheets

The paper Necessary for printing 2,000 impressions on the best Colombier paper, according to this plan, will be 95 Reams — but for fear the Sizes of the plates should not have been ascertaind with precision — it woud be better to order 100 Reams — if this plan is adopted. —

There is however another plan, which seems to be very much the Wish of Mr Webber & the other Artists — & that is, to print all the 65 plates on 1/2 Sheets — This plan woud undoubtedly make the plates look more beautifull, & uniform — particularly to those who will do them up seperate from their book — The Argument against it is — that it will make upwards of £200 difference in the expence — For by this method 130 Reams of Colombier paper will be necessary —

The following statement will give some Idea of the difference
    It is conjectured that the paper with Duty, Freight and all expences will come to something about £7 ⅌ Ream
        That price for — 130 Reams is £910 —
        And — for — 100 Reams is — 700

                        £ 210. difference

It seems universally allowd that English paper is the best for printing the charts —

In the end, a large number of engravers were used to prepare the illustrations for the official voyage account. This leaf shows whether an original work in the voyage artists' hand existed, whether it had been copied at a smaller size, and the great range of amounts paid for the work. No doubt the experience of each engraver and the complexity of the job was taken into account.

Crowned and carried aloft by the allegorical figures of Britannia and Fame, Cook ascends to heaven from Kealakekua Bay while his companions fire from small boats at the natives on the shore. A painting of the scene may have concluded the 1785 pantomime *Omai*, the libretto at the point noting, 'A Grand Painting descends'. A contemporary newspaper account recorded: 'The entertainment concludes with an apotheosis of Captain Cook, crowned by Fame and Britannia, with the medallions of several celebrated English naval officers in the back ground.'

No in the Publication	original Drawing	reduced Drawing		Engravers name		
4	✓	✓	Christmas harbour in Kerguelens Land	Newton	31	10
6	✓	✓	Man of Van Diemens Land	J. Caldwell	36	15
7	✓	✓	Woman of Van Diemens Land	J. Caldwell	42	—
8	✓	o	Opossum of Van Diemens Land	P. Mazell	10	10
10	✓	✓	Inside of a Hippah in New Zeland	B.T. Pouncey	47	5
11	✓		Man of Mangea	W Sharp	26	5
13	✓	✓	View at Anemoka	W. Byrne	94	10
14	✓	✓	Reception of Capt. Cook at Hapaee	Heath	84	—
15	✓	✓	a boxing metch at Hapaee	J Taylor	31	10
16	✓	✓	night Dance by men at Hapaee	W Sharp	94	10
17	✓	✓	night Dance by women at Hapaee	W Sharp	94	10
18	o	✓	Poulaho king of the Friendly Isles	J Hall	36	15
20	✓	✓	Poulaho drinking Cava	Wm Sharp	73	10
21	✓	✓	a Fiatooka or Morai in Tongataboo	Wm Ellis	47	5
22	Roll	✓	Natche a Ceremony in Tongataboo figures	J Hall	94	10
22		✓	——————— Landscape	J. Middemer		
23	✓	✓	a woman of Eaoo	J Hall	36	15
25	✓	✓	a Human sacrifice in Otaheite	W. Woollett	157	10
26	✓	✓	The body of Tee as preserved after death	W. Byrne	52	10
27	✓	✓	A Young woman of Otaheite bringing a present	F. Bartolozzi	52	10
28	✓	✓	a Dance in Otaheite	J.K. Sherwin	126	—
29	✓	✓	a Young woman dancing in Otaheite	J.K. Sherwin	36	15
31	✓	✓	a view in Huaheine	W. Byrne	63	5
33	✓	✓	a Morai in Atooi	Lerpinière	31	10
34	✓	✓	inside of a house in the morai at atooi	Scott	10	10
35	✓	✓	inland view at atooi	J. Middeman	73	10
38	o	✓	a men of Northa sound	W Sharp	26	5
39	✓	✓	a women of Northa sound	W. Sharp	26	5
40	✓	o	various articles in Northa sound	J. Record	5	5
41	✓	✓	view of habitations in Northa sound	J. Smith	52	10
42	✓	✓	Inside of a house in Northa sound	W Sharp	63	—
43	✓	o	sea otter	Mazell	10	10
45	✓	✓	Snug corner Cove	W. Ellis	63	—
					1604	10

Henry Roberts (1757–1796)
A General Chart Exhibiting the Discoveries Made by Captn James Cook in This and His Two Preceeding Voyages, with the Tracks of the Ships under His Command 1780s
hand-coloured engraving
Tooley Collection (Maps), National Library of Australia, Canberra, MAP T 331

Lieutenant Roberts explained how this map came about:

> Soon after our departure from England, I was instructed by Captain Cook to complete a map of the world as a general chart, from the best materials he was in possession of for that purpose; and before his death this business was in great measure accomplished … But on our return home, when the fruits of our voyage were ordered by the Lords Commissioners of the Admiralty to be published, the care of the general chart being consigned to me, I was directed to prepare it from the latest and best authorities; and also to introduce Captain Cook's three successive tracks; that all his discoveries, and the different routes he had taken might appear together.

William Bligh, later of *Bounty* fame, was master of the *Resolution* and a skilled mapmaker. He complained that Roberts received much of the credit for mapmaking on the third voyage, claiming that he himself had drawn most of the original charts.

The APOTHEOSIS of CAPTAIN COOK.

From a Design of P.J.De Loutherbourg, R.A. The View of KARAKAKOOA BAY
Is from a Drawing by John Webber, R.A (the last he made) in the Collection of M.r G.Baker.

London, Pub.d Jan.y 20. 1794, by J. Thane, Spur Street, Leicester Square.

Exhibiting the DISCOVERIES made by Capt.ⁿ JAMES COOK in this and

By Lieut.ᵗ Rob[...]

PART OF GREENLAND

ARCTIC SEA

NORTH CAPE

NOVA ZEMBLA

LAPLAND

SAMOJED

TUNGUSI

JAKUTI

NORWAY

SWEDEN

FINLAND

ARCHANGEL

SIBERIA

TUNGUSI

ICELAND

NORTH

BRITISH ISLES

ATLANTIC

POLAND

GERMANY

FRANCE

HUNGARY

MOSCOW

EUROPE

RUSSIA

WESTERN TARTARY

KALMUCKS

KALMUCKS

MONGOLS

EASTERN TARTARY

MANSHURS

SPAIN

TURKEY IN EUROPE

CASPIAN SEA

KOBI or Sandy Desert called SHAMO by the Chinese MONGOLS

WHANG HAY

ITALY

MEDITERRANEAN SEA

TURKEY IN ASIA

ARMENIA

BUKARIA

KOBI or Sandy Desert

THIBET

NAPAUL

CHINA

OCEAN

MOROCCO

ALGIERS

TRIPOLI

PERSIA

MAKRAN

DELHI

OUDE

SINDY

BERAR

HINDOOSTAN

BOOTAN

BAY of BENGAL

QUEICHEW

QUANSI

SIAM

PHILIPINE ISLES

SAHARA or Desert of Barbary

TROPIC OF CANCER

NUBIA

EGYPT

ARABIA

NEGROLAND

ABYSSINIA

AJAN

LACCADIVE ISLES

MALDIVE ISLES

THE Isles

CEYLON

TONKIN

BORNEO

CANARY ISLES

CAPE VERD IS.

GUINEA

AFRICA

CONGO

ZANGUEBAR

INDIAN OCEAN

SOUTH ATLANTIC OCEAN

ST HELENA

ASCENSION I.

MADAGASCAR

MOZAMBIQUE

HOTTENTOTS

CAPE GOOD HOPE

NEW HOLLAND

Land of Peter Nuyts discover'd 1627

OCEAN

ISLE of DESOLATION

SANDWICH LAND

Southern Thule

OCEAN

THE ANTAR[CTIC]

EXPLANATION.
This shews the Endeavours Track in the Years 1768.1769.1770.&1771.
Resolution's First Voyage in 1772.1773.1774.&1775.
Resolution's Second Voyage in 1776.1777.1778.1779.&1780.

E. Longitude from the Meridian

...CTIC SEA

NORTH

ARCTIC CIRCLE

COPPER INDIANS

THE SEA

Coppermine R.

BAFFINS BAY

BAFFINS STRAITS

CUMBERLAND ISLES

DAVIS STRAITS

GREENLAND

NORTHERN INDIANS

DOG RIB'D INDIANS

ATHAPESCOW INDIANS

HUDSONS BAY

ISLE OF GOOD FORTUNE

LABRADOR OR ESKIMAUX OR NEW BRITAIN

NORTH

NEW SOUTH WALES

BRISTOL BAY

NORTH

Q. Charlottes Islands

NORTH

AMERICA

PACIFIC

ATLANTIC

UNITED STATES

NORTH CAROLINA

SOUTH CAROLINA

NEW MEXICO

LOUISIANA

GULF of MEXICO

Mexico

Acapulco

CARIBBEAN SEA

OCEAN

TIERRA FIRMA

NEW GRANADA

GALLAPAGOS ISLES

Isles known by the Spaniards

SOUTH

COUNTRY of AMAZONS

AMERICA

PARAGUAY

Rio Janeiro

TROPIC OF CAPRICORN

SOUTH

ATLANTIC

OCEAN

NEW HEBRIDES

NEW CALEDONIA

ISLES

NEW ZEELAND

SOUTH

PACIFIC

OCEAN

CAPE HORN

Falklands Isles

Isle of Georgia

ATLANTIC OCEAN

EQUINOCTIAL LINE

...CTIC CIRCLE

...TIC OCEAN

Reference to the Colours.
The British discoveries in the Pacific Ocean &c. Red.
The Russian D.s on the N.E. Coast of Asia & N.W. Coast of America Blue.

157

8. COOK AFTER COOK

As Cook's three great voyages faded from living memory, the man achieved legendary status: a revered figure who could do no wrong. If there was any unease in Britain about his achievements, it was limited to those with a close understanding of the impact the voyages had had on the peoples of the Pacific. In Australia, popular celebrations led to the erection of Cook monuments and to the persistent and widespread belief that Captain Cook discovered Australia. Gradually, as the bicentenary of his death approached in 1970, authoritative editions of his journals, and detailed studies of the art and artefacts from the voyages, revealed a more nuanced story.

Perhaps because of the rich historical sources, both written and physical, Cook has always been a key figure in popular history. He has come to be seen as a symbol of the 'great white man' in European history. As such, Cook is perhaps an ideal figure through which eighteenth- and early nineteenth-century European notions of civilisation and colonisation, as part of a broader program of empire, could be challenged. Cook changed the European world through his drive to 'discover'. He and his men had significant interactions with Indigenous peoples across the Pacific, some of which were destructive. In parts of the Pacific, the voyages led to events which undermined sovereignty and initiated human tragedy. Elsewhere, Cook's legacy has been woven more readily into the fabric of official history and identity. The question of how perceptions of Cook have evolved over the decades since the 1770s continues to inspire artists and fuel debate.

Staffordshire Figurine of Captain James Cook 1845–51
Pictures Collection, National Library of Australia, Canberra, PIC
CZ 1/4/3 #PIC/20246

Cook's image was revisited throughout the nineteenth century. This
porcelain figurine, one of the finest of the Staffordshire series made
at the Alpha factory, is based on the 1776 Nathaniel Dance portrait
of Cook. The map he holds in that painting, however, has become a
manuscript here. There is some suggestion that the Alpha figurines
may have been made for display in the 1851 Great Exhibition at
London's Crystal Palace.

Voyages to the Southern Hemisphere; or Nature Explored …
London: R. Snagg, c. 1775
Petherick Collection (Australian Printed), National Library of
Australia, Canberra, SR COOK 358

The earliest known children's book relating to Australia, *Voyages to
the Southern Hemisphere* is written in the form of a catechism with
questions and answers presenting the *Endeavour* voyage and its
immediate British predecessors to a young audience.

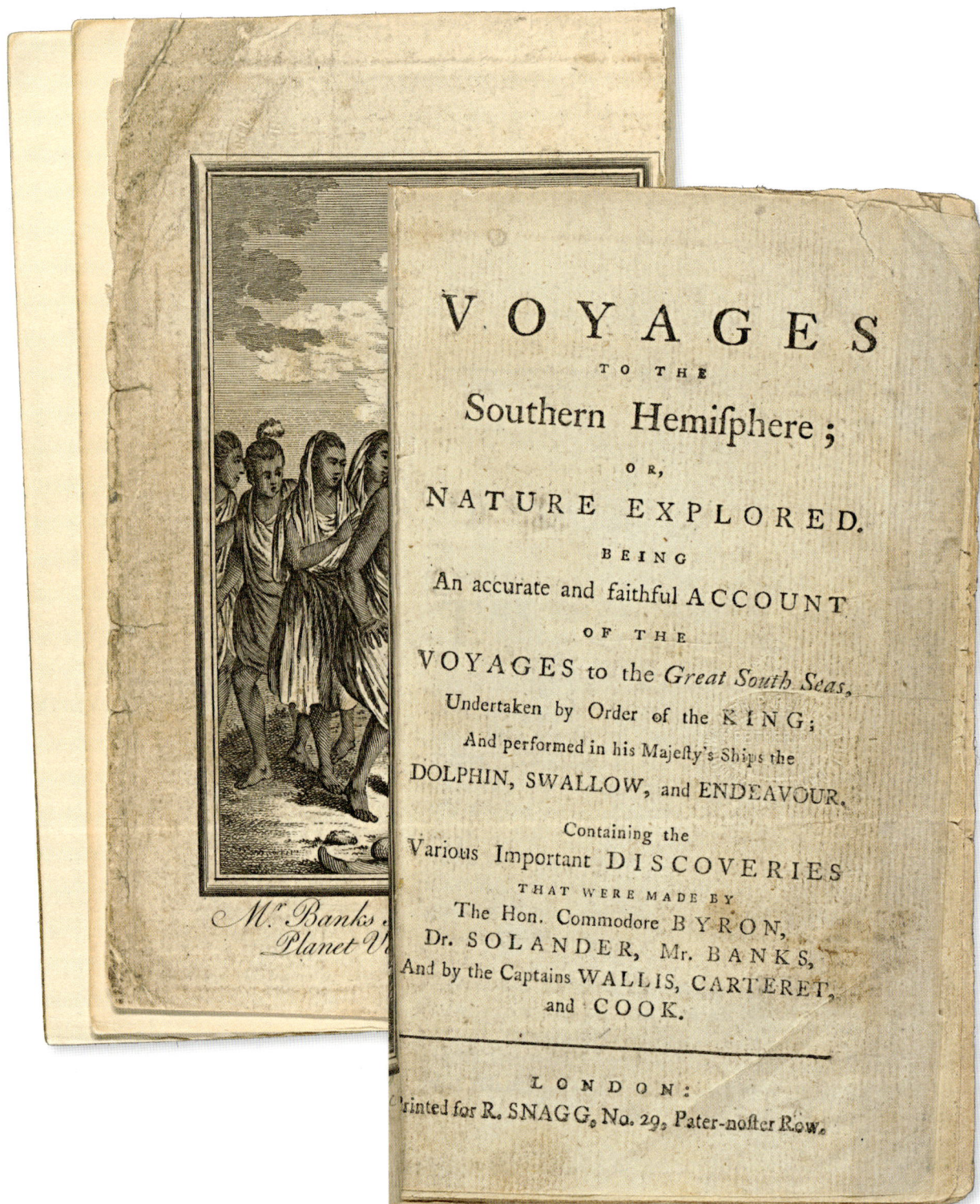

Mr Banks
Planet V...

VOYAGES

TO THE

Southern Hemisphere;

OR,

NATURE EXPLORED.

BEING

An accurate and faithful ACCOUNT

OF THE

VOYAGES to the *Great South Seas,*

Undertaken by Order of the KING;

And performed in his Majesty's Ships the

DOLPHIN, SWALLOW, and ENDEAVOUR.

Containing the

Various Important DISCOVERIES

THAT WERE MADE BY

The Hon. Commodore BYRON,
Dr. SOLANDER, Mr. BANKS,
And by the Captains WALLIS, CARTERET,
and COOK.

LONDON:

Printed for R. SNAGG, No. 29, Pater-noster Row.

TOP

Alan Tucker (b. 1952)
Too Many Captain Cooks
Norwood, South Australia: Omnibus Books, 1994
Australian Printed Collection, National Library of Australia,
Canberra, NLq 994.0049915 T891
Courtesy Alan Tucker

Over the years, many children's books about Cook and his voyages
have been published, many of which tell the story of his *Endeavour
voyage* and his 'discovery' of Australia. In more recent years,
however, Australian children's literature has been extending the
traditional narrative, and stories have appeared that highlight the
Indigenous narrative surrounding Cook; for example, Tucker's *Too
Many Captain Cooks* and *The Aboriginal Children's History of Australia*
(1977), written and illustrated by Australia's Aboriginal children.

The National Library of Australia houses a collection of children's
literature on Cook and his voyages that reveals how he has been
remembered, celebrated and reinterpreted over the past 250 years.

BOTTOM

Michael Salmon (b. 1949)
G'day Captain Cook: Welcome to Australia, Colouring Book
Templestowe, Victoria: Lamont Books, 1988
Kerry White Collection (Australian Printed), National Library
of Australia, Canberra, KWp 430
Courtesy Michael Salmon

Published in the year of the bicentenary of the arrival of the First
Fleet, this colouring book for children highlights the increasing
recognition of Aboriginal history.

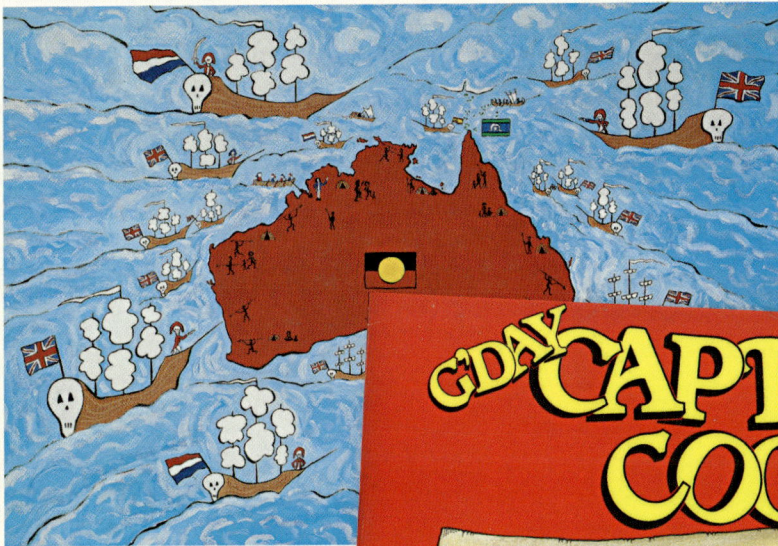

TOO MANY CAPTAIN COOKS

ALAN

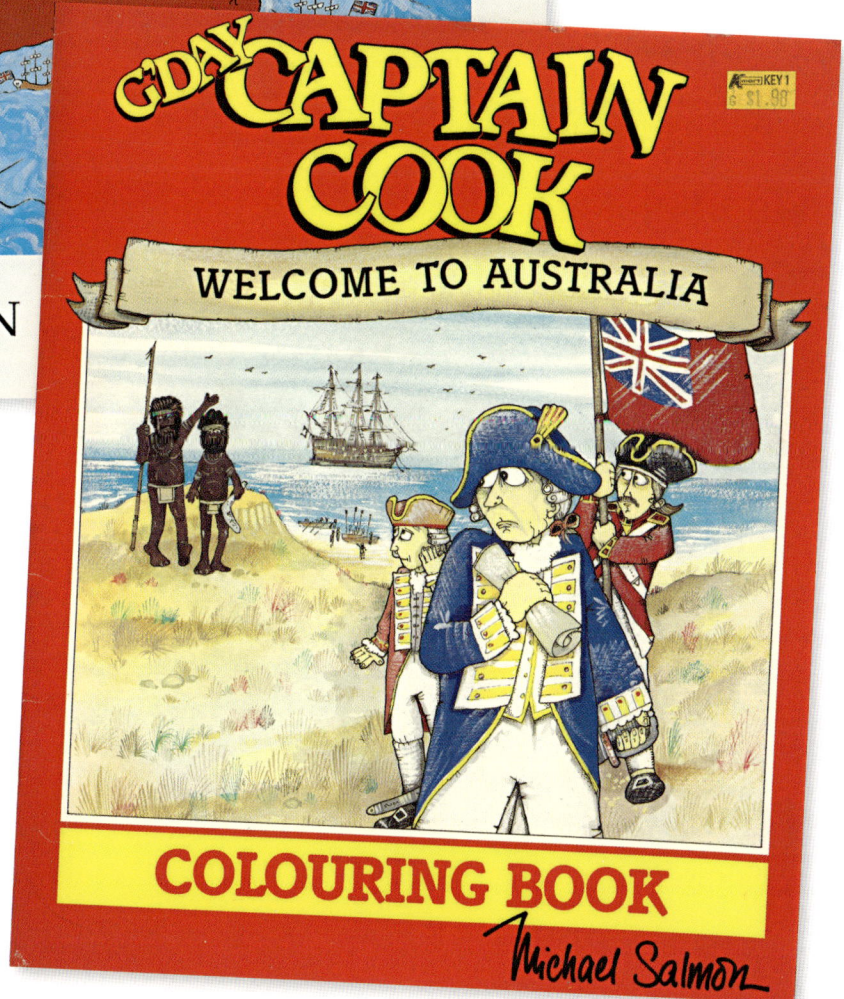

G'DAY CAPTAIN COOK
WELCOME TO AUSTRALIA
COLOURING BOOK
Michael Salmon

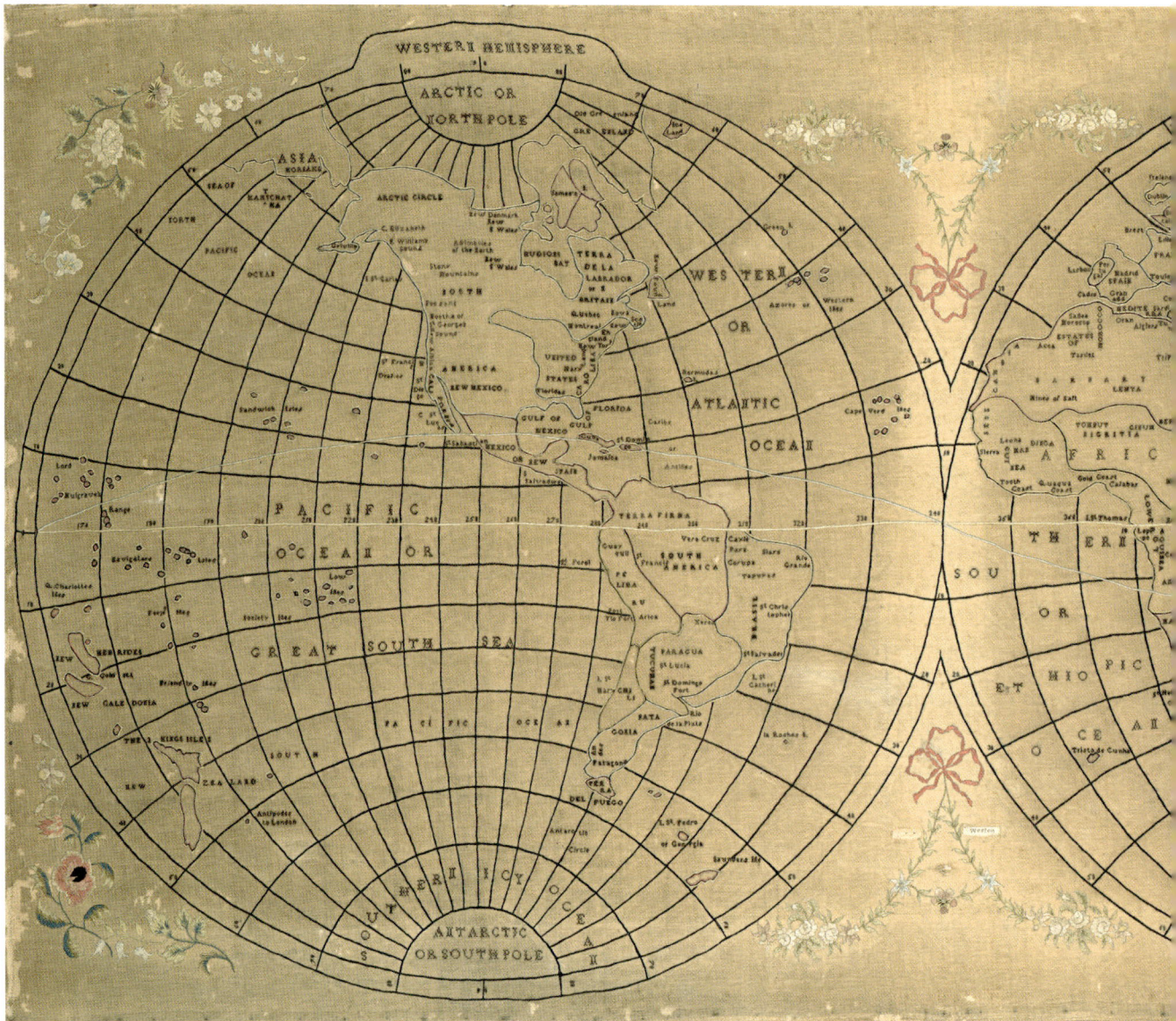

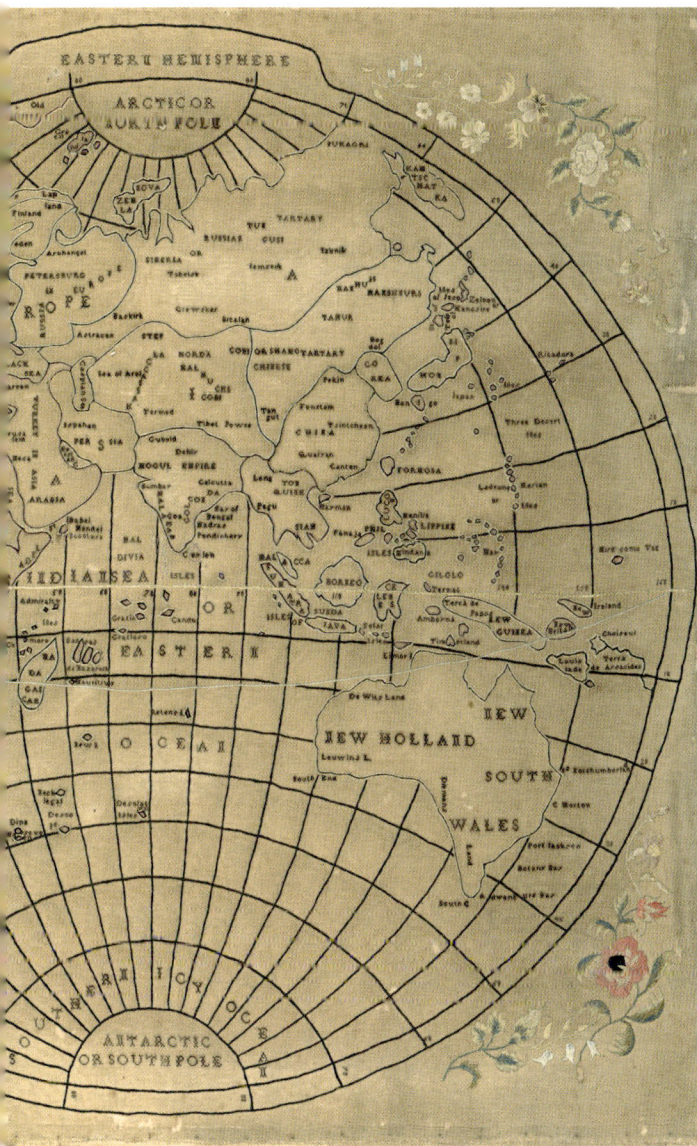

Miss Weston
Embroidered Map of the World Featuring Places Mapped on Cook's Voyages c. 1790
Maps Collection, National Library of Australia, Canberra, MAP RM 4889

Cook's achievements soon became a favourite subject in the home, general education and popular culture. Many objects invited British people to revisit the European discovery of distant lands and cultures, and the successes of His Majesty's ships. The double hemispherical world map allowed the Cook voyages their broadest scope in educational tools such as 'dissected puzzles' (now known as jigsaw puzzles) and embroidery samplers.

Matthew Darly (publisher, c. 1720–1780)
The Botanic Macaroni, The Fly Catching Macaroni
and The Simpling Macaroni 1772
Rex Nan Kivell Collection (Pictures), National Library
of Australia, Canberra, PIC Drawer 7261 #U6305 NK5003,
PIC Drawer 7261 #U6303 NK5004 and PIC Drawer 7261
#U7126 NK5005

In the early 1770s, London printers Matthew and Mary Darly
began a series of prints attacking men dubbed 'macaronis',
after the Italian pasta. Though hard to define, these were
often men who had travelled and had some sort of driving
foreign interest or passion. Two figures (below and top right)
can be identified as Banks, while the third (bottom right) is
Daniel Solander.

The BOTANIC MACARONI

The FLY CATCHING MACARONI.
I rove from Pole to Pole, you ask me why,
I tell you Truth, to catch a _____ Fly.

The SIMPLING MACARONI.
Like Soland-Goose from frozen Zone I wander,
On shallow Banks grows fat, Sol . . . . .

George Molnar (1910–1998)
'All this pommy showing-off. Why couldn't Australia have been discovered by an Australian?' 1970
Pryor Collection of Cartoons and Drawings (Pictures), National Library of Australia, Canberra, PIC Drawer 9381 #PIC/3705/11

Australian cartoonists have found the subject of Cook a rich vein for humour, which is hardly surprising considering that his name is more widely known than many other figures in Australian history. Molnar had been active in the Sydney University Libertarian Society and the 'Sydney Push'. The Cook bicentenary in 1970 galvanised those who saw it as another representation of British political authority over Australians.

"*All this pommy showing-off. Why couldn't Australia have been discovered by an Australian?*"

165

Arthur Horner (1916–1997)
'This is the place for a cottage' 1980
Arthur Horner archive of cartoons (Pictures), National Library
of Australia, Canberra, PIC Drawer 54 #PIC/14175/5c
Courtesy of the artist's family

This comes from a series of cartoons on Australian history by
Arthur Horner published in *The Age* newspaper in Melbourne
between 1980 and 1981. It appeared with the caption: 'And last
the enlightened British, star-gazing, map-making, and gathering
wildflowers for the greater glory of Kew Gardens; their leader the
modest Captain Cook, who gave his name to a cottage.' What was
believed to be Captain Cook's childhood Yorkshire home was
purchased by Russell Grimwade and moved, brick by brick, all
150 tonnes of it, to Australia in 1934; today it sits in Melbourne's
Fitzroy Gardens. There is little evidence that it was in fact Cook's
home, though it is possible he visited it in 1772.

Geoff Pryor (b. 1944)
'Let's hope the natives are friendly' … 'Well—I won't be too sorry if they're not!' 1998
Pictures Collection, National Library of Australia, Canberra, PIC Drawer 10631 #PIC/10753/262

In this Australia Day cartoon, long time *Canberra Times* cartoonist Geoff Pryor takes aim at the refusal of then Prime Minister John Howard (shown dressed as Cook at Botany Bay) to say 'Sorry' to Indigenous Australians for their past treatment, preferring to express regret.

George M. Cohan (1878–1942)
'If Captain Cook should come to life' c. 1909
Music Collection, National Library of Australia, Canberra,
MUS N mba 782.14 C678

'If Captain Cook should come to life' was a local addition, composed
by the famous American songwriter, to the hit musical *The Girl
Behind the Counter* (first performed in London in 1906). Written
in a new era of British nationalism (and rivalry with Germany),
George M. Cohan's words asked Australians to ponder Cook's
reaction to the dangers that beset the motherland. He was in no
doubt that Cook would 'find us in the lead with the boys of the
bull dog breed'.

Miriam Hyde (1913–2005)
Captain Cook Sketchbook: A Suite of Five Pieces for Pianoforte
Melbourne: Allans Music Australia, c. 1970
Music Collection, National Library of Australia, Canberra,
MUS N m 786/20994

Some of Australia's best-known composers have turned their hand to Cook, among them Alfred Hill, Dulcie Holland, Anne Boyd and Miriam Hyde. The earliest efforts date to the late nineteenth century, with anniversaries such as the bicentenary of Cook's landing at Botany Bay attracting greatest attention.

IMPERIAL EDITION No. 1090

Captain Cook Sketchbook
A Suite of Five Pieces for Pianoforte

By MIRIAM HYDE

Southward Bound

Merry Sailor

Becalmed in the Tropics

The First Corroboree

Hoisting the Flag

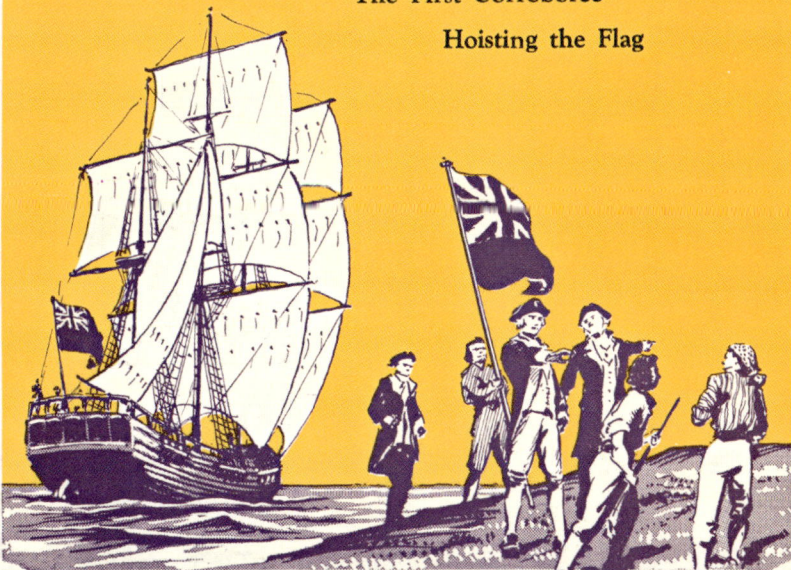

ALLANS MUSIC (AUSTRALIA) PTY. LTD.
MELBOURNE ADELAIDE HOBART GEELONG BENDIGO LAUNCESTON

Printed in Australia

55c

Australian National Travel Association
Smith and Julius Studios, Sydney
*Australia's 150th Anniversary, Sydney 1938: Pageantry
and Carnival 26 January – 25 April* 1938
Pictures Collection, National Library of Australia, Canberra,
PIC Poster Drawer 26

This poster was produced for celebrations surrounding the 150th
anniversary of the arrival of Captain Arthur Phillip and the First
Fleet at Sydney Cove in 1788. With his back to the viewer, a Cook-
like figure oversees the scene, which includes a depiction of the
landing of Phillip and his men, with two Aboriginal men placed off
to the side. There are fireworks over the Sydney Harbour Bridge,
which had opened just six years earlier.

James Northfield (artist, 1887–1973); F.W. Niven Pty Ltd (printer)
Discover Australia 1950s
Melbourne: Australian National Publicity Association
Pictures Collection, National Library of Australia, Canberra,
PIC Poster Drawer 199
© James Northfield Heritage Art Trust

Playing on the popular idea that Cook discovered Australia, this
poster encourages overseas tourists to visit Australia. The tag
line proclaims that 'Australia's history began when Captain Cook
anchored in Botany Bay in 1770'. A variation on this poster was used
to advertise the airline Qantas. Northfield was one of the country's
great graphic artists of the twentieth century.

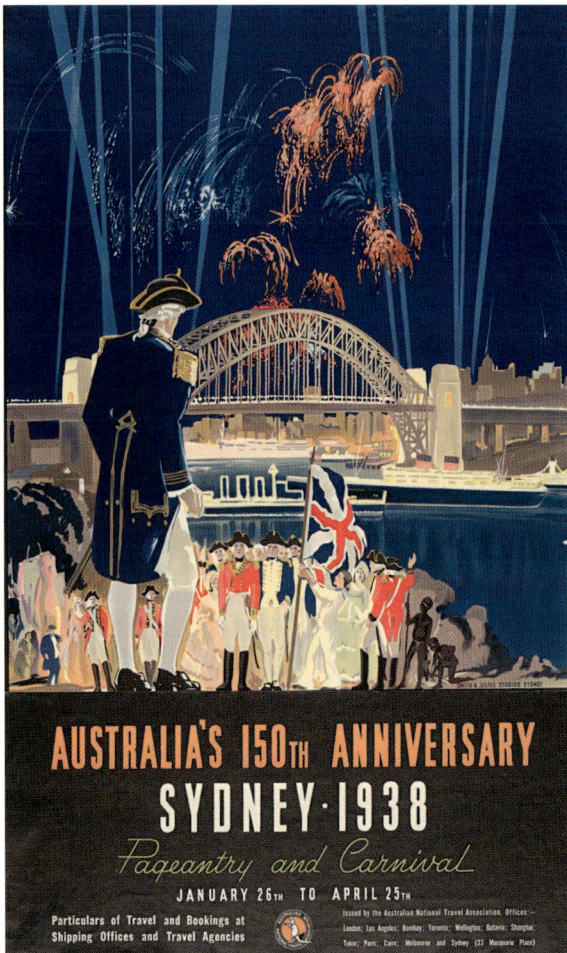

Bill Brindle (d. 1984)
Re-enactment of the Landing of Captain Cook at Kurnell, in Botany Bay 1970
Pictures Collection, National Library of Australia, Canberra, PIC Box PIC/9907 #PIC/9907

The re-enactment was the climax of nationwide Cook celebrations that coincided with promotion of Australian history to a receptive public. On 29 April 1970 the tall ship *Monte Cristo*, badged for the occasion as *New Endeavour*, sailed into Botany Bay. Several 'warriors' waited ashore, including Aboriginal actors performing 'domestic scenes' of fishing. The re-enactment was disrupted by university students, one of whom was dressed in a Captain Cook costume. They arrived at the landing site in a speedboat and took possession of Australia 'in the name of George the Third and Sydney University'.

171

Antill's Corroboree, G'day Digger, Song of Hagar 1970
Pictures Collection, National Library of Australia, Canberra,
PIC Poster Drawer 5

During 1970 the bicentenary of Cook's landings along Australia's east coast was widely celebrated across the country, but especially at Kurnell, where Cook landed. The local council built an amphitheatre in Cronulla's Gunnamatta Park where, in March 1970, the Australian Contemporary Dance Company presented a triple bill, with African-American dancer and choreographer Ronne Arnold in the lead role. Australian composer John Antill (1904–1986) composed the music for all three ballets. *Corroboree* had premiered in 1954, before Queen Elizabeth II, on her first visit to Australia.

The monument commemorating the 1970 bicentenary and the
visit of Queen Elizabeth II to Kingscliff stated, 'Captain James Cook
claimed the whole of the east coast of Australia for Great Britain
on 22 August 1770, naming eastern Australia, New South Wales'.
Similar sentiments had been etched into the memories of previous
generations at earlier commemorations, and by 1970 they were even
used as part of advertising campaigns.

The enthusiasm for Cook celebrations was considerable,
and committees formed in every Australian state and territory.
In addition to the Royal Tour, many monuments and statues were
erected, a commemorative 50-cent piece was coined, medals and
stamps were issued; there were exhibitions, publications and public
talks, and sailing ships arrived from several countries to take part
in the festivities. Airline advertisements in places such as the United
States announced: 'Colorful observances commemorating the great
British navigator's historic explorations in 1770' would be held in
Sydney and 'numerous other picturesque Australian, cities and towns.'

FLY **ANSETT** ▲
AIRLINES OF AUSTRALIA

Jam.f.Cook

CAPTAIN COOK BI~CENTENARY CELEBRATIONS   **1770-1970**

NEW SOUTH WALES, AUSTRALIA

Bookshelf of Works Drawn from the National Library of Australia

Cook's voyages remained a key moment in exploration history, and the man himself a revered figure in the pantheon of British heroes and explorers, well into the twentieth century. The authoritative edition of Cook's journals did not appear until the volumes by J.C. Beaglehole were published in the years leading up to the bicentenary of the *Endeavour* voyage.

Cook became well known to Australians through a variety of publications, languages and styles—from dense scholarly tomes to highly illustrated popular works. The approaches to writing about Cook embraced a range of studies that dealt with navigation, cartography and voyaging; his leadership and discoveries; his life and times; and what was, in the view of some writers, his murder.

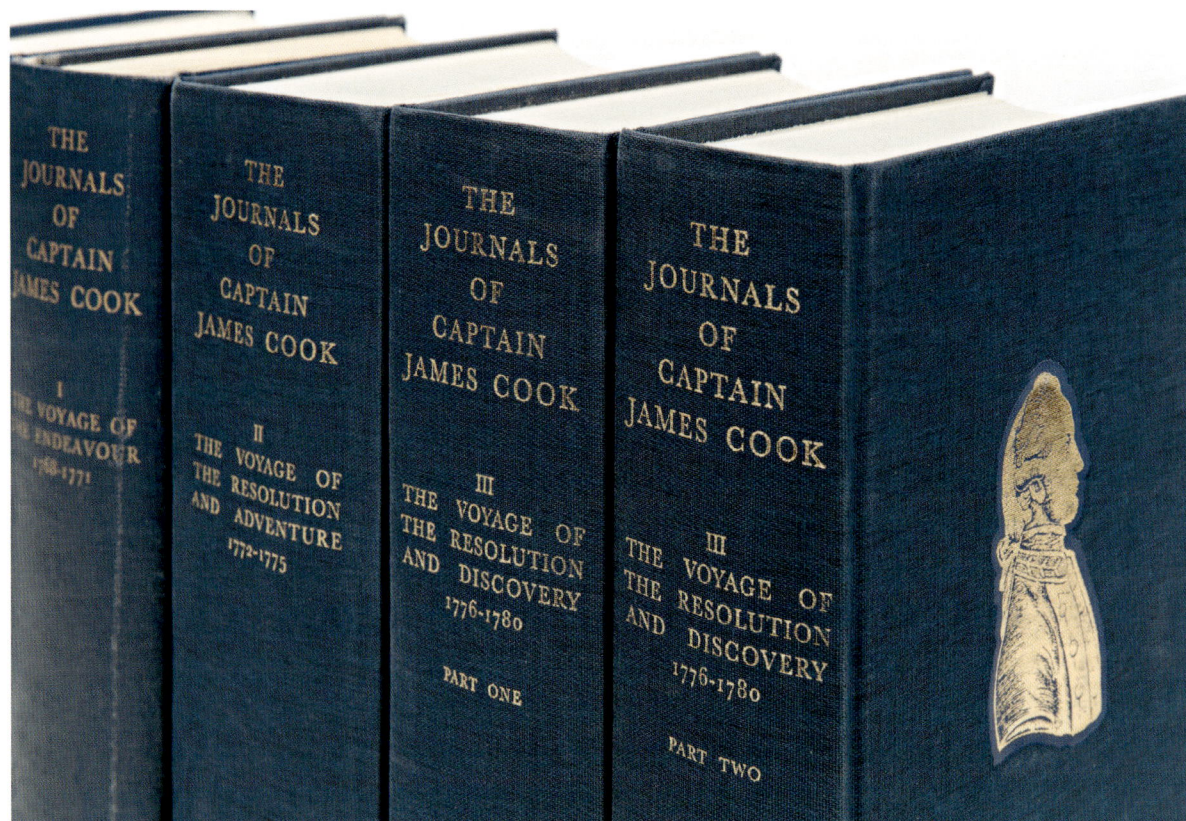

Boomali Aboriginal Artists Co-operative
Captain Cook 1988
Pictures Collection, National Library of Australia, Canberra,
PIC Poster Drawer 1
© Paddy Wainburranga Fordham/Copyright Agency, 2018

The legacy of Cook's *Endeavour* voyage up in the east coast of
Australia in 1770 is complex, and is sometimes tied to the arrival
of the First Fleet in Botany Bay in January 1788. This poster shows
a bark painting and narrative of Captain Cook by Paddy Fordham
Wainburranga, a Rembarrnga man, and was produced as part of the

We Have Survived series. Produced by Australian Aboriginal artists,
the series of works depicts the experiences and survival of Australia's
First Nations people since the arrival of the First Fleet.

They wanted to take all of Australia.
They wanted it, they wanted the whole lot of this country. All the new
people wanted anything they could get.
They could shoot people.
New Captain Cook mob!
But now we've got our culture back.
That's all. That's the story now.

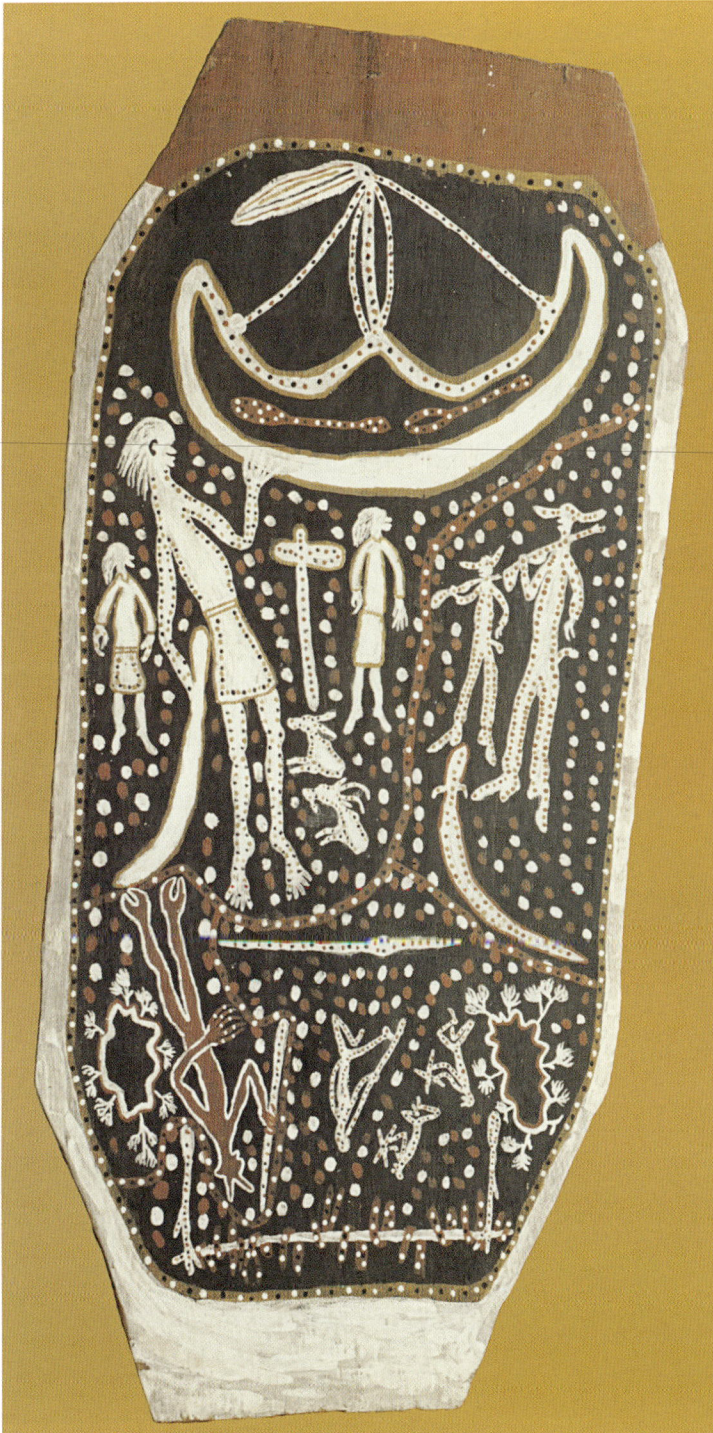

Captain Cook

This painting is Captain Cook's song the way the Rembarrnga people know it from a long time ago.

Captain Cook was around during the time of Satan. Everybody knows Captain Cook. Old people, not young people. You've got to have a lot of learning to know Captain Cook. More culture. I can sing it now for this bark painting. This is the way his song goes.

Captain Cook came from Mosquito Island, which is east of New Guinea. He came with his two wives, a donkey and a nanny goat.

He was a really hard man, he had a hard job to do when he came to Sydney Harbour. He had his business building his *barrupa* — his boat.

In more recent times when boats came, it came from *murldi* — Macassans in white man's language. But the first boat came from Captain Cook.

From the earliest days Satan lived there too. We call Satan *ngayang*. It's the same as a devil. He lived on the other side of the harbour on Sydney Island. The other side of the harbour is called *Wanambal*.

Satan has feet like a bullock's. He's got horns, see? He had long nails on his fingers. He also had a devil bone to fight with.

Captain Cook worked by himself on his boat, he used to always be working on his boat.

He would always come back and have his dinner after working on his boat, then he would go to sleep.

But he didn't know that the *ngayang* was always sneaking up behind his back while he was working. The devil had been talking to his two wives.

One day Satan came behind his back to the wives and said: "I'm going to kill Captain Cook and take the two of you over to that other island. See over there? You two have to come over with me."

Satan said to them: "You dig a well and cover me up with dirt. When he comes back to eat his food I'll come out behind him, out of the ground."

When Captain Cook came back to eat his supper, he didn't know. And then Satan, *ngayang*, came out and poked Captain Cook in the back with his bone.

Captain Cook said: "I know you. You're Satan behind my back. I'll turn around and look at you Satan."

Satan said: "I'll fight you and kill you and take your two wives."

"All right. We'll fight," said Captain Cook.

Satan said, "Have you got power (magic)? If you want to fight me you have to be a clever man!"

"No, I haven't got power." Captain Cook only had a stone axe. "You put that bone down, and I'll put down the axe. We'll wrestle, hand to hand."

So they fought. At first Satan was winning. He threw Captain Cook against the boat he had built. But then Captain Cook grabbed the devil by his throat, he wrapped his arm around his neck and broke it. The *ngayang* couldn't move. He was dead.

Captain Cook then grabbed the devil by the scruff of his neck and through his legs and chucked him into the ground — into a hole — as a punishment.

The devil was in the hole in the ground. The hole in the ground is this side of the water. Here.

And motor cars go through there now and come out on the other side of the Harbour at *Wanambal*.

After the fight, Captain Cook went back to his own country, to Mosquito Island. We don't know what happened there. Maybe all his family were jealous.

But they attacked him with a spear. That's the spear in the painting. His own people attacked him.

Captain Cook came back to Sydney Harbour then, and he died from the spear wounds. The old man was sick and he sat down with everything he had and died. And then he was buried there in Sydney Harbour. Underneath. On the island.

I've finished with the story of old Captain Cook. I'm talking now about all the new Captain Cooks.

When the old people died, other people started thinking they could make Captain Cook another way. New people. Maybe all his sons.

Too many Captain Cooks.

They started shooting people then. New Captain Cook people. Those are the people that made war when Captain Cook died; because they didn't care, they didn't know, all those young people.

They are the ones who have been stealing all the women and killing people. They have made war. Warmakers, those new Captain Cooks. They fought all the wars. Warmakers. They fought.

The olden time Captain Cook is dead but all the new people have made trouble.

That old Captain Cook died a long time ago, but new Captain Cooks shot people.

They killed the women, these new people. They called themselves "New Captain Cooks".

I've got to tell you about the warmaking people. The ones who made war. The new ones. Mr White, Bill Harney, Mr Sweeney.

They just went after women. All the New Captain Cooks fought the people. They shot people. Not old Captain Cook: he didn't interfere or make a war.

That last war and the second war. They fought us. And then they made a new thing called "welfare".

All the New Captain Cook mob came and called themselves "welfare mob".

They wanted to take all of Australia.

They wanted it, they wanted the whole lot of this country. All the new people wanted anything they could get.

They could shoot people.

New Captain Cook mob!

But now we've got our culture back.

That's all. That's the story now.

PRODUCED AS PART OF THE 'WE HAVE SURVIVED' SERIES WITH ASSISTANCE FROM THE NORTHERN LAND COUNCIL & THE CENTRAL LAND COUNCIL, 1988

Regis Lansac (b. 1947)
Anti-bicentenary Demonstration, Sydney January 1988
Pictures Collection, National Library of Australia, Canberra,
PIC/3797/5 LOC Drawer PIC 3797
Courtesy Regis Lansac

On Australia Day 26 January 1988, more than 40,000 people
took part in a march in Sydney (and in other Australian centres),
highlighting the rights and recognition of Australian Aboriginal and
Torres Strait Islander peoples. The march challenged existing ideas
about what Australia Day represented. In addition to focusing on
land rights, the event came in the midst of the Royal Commission
into Aboriginal Deaths in Custody, and drew to people's attention to
the current state of Indigenous health and welfare.

One of the banners visible in Lansac's photograph repeats a major
recurring slogan in Australian Aboriginal protest: 'White Aust.
has a black history'. Chanting for land rights, the protesters marched
from Redfern Park to a public rally at Hyde Park, and then on to
Sydney Harbour, where several prominent Aboriginal leaders and
activists spoke. The march challenged existing ideas about what
Australia Day represented. In addition to focusing attention on
poor health, education and welfare, the event came in the midst
of the Royal Commission into Aboriginal Deaths in Custody to
investigate the causes of deaths of Aboriginal people held in state
and territory prisons.

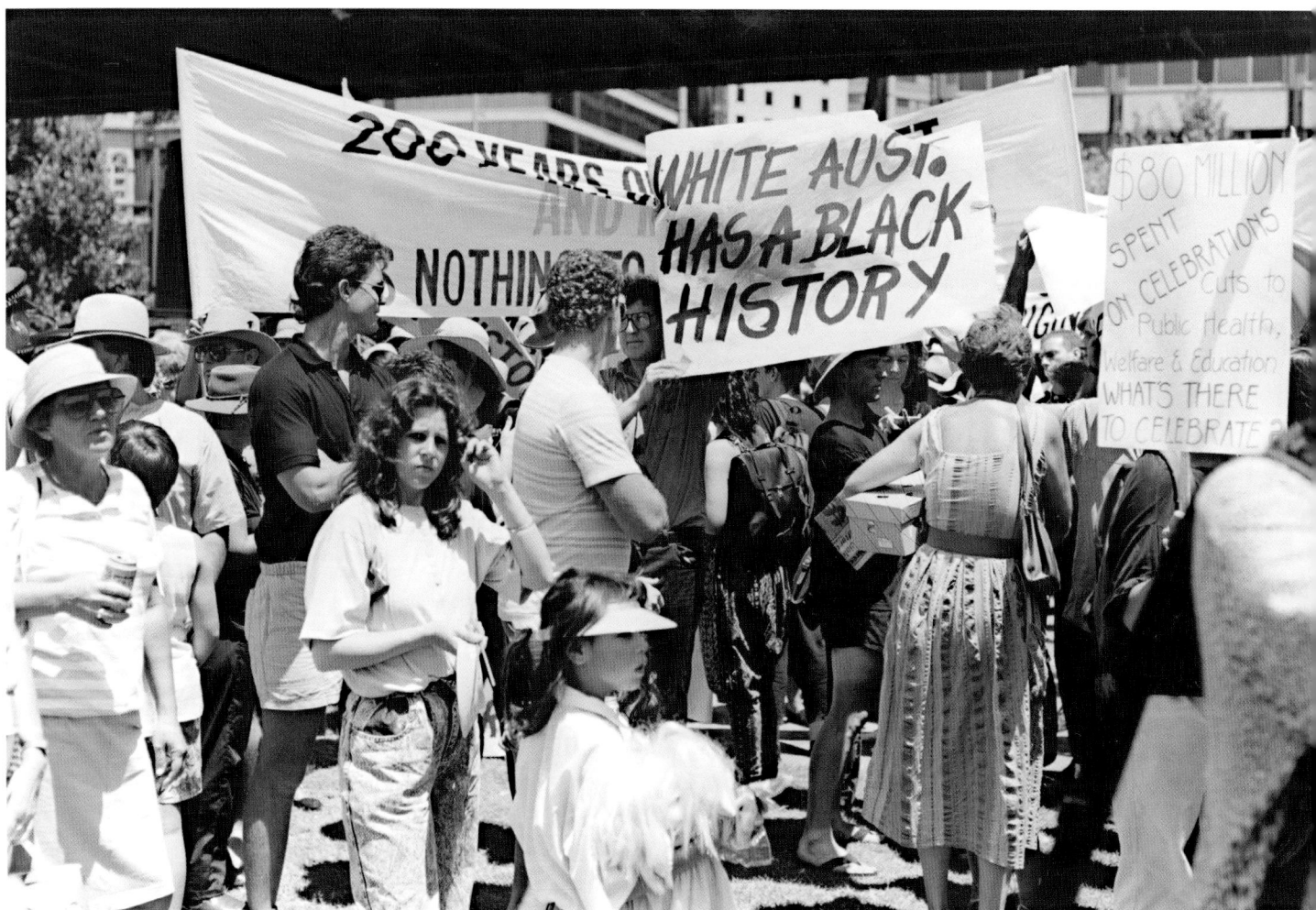

Edward Koiki Mabo (1936–1992)
Map of the East North East Shoreline of Murray Island, Looking West South West, Showing E. Mabo's Portions
Papers of Bryan Keon-Cohen: The Mabo Case (Manuscripts), National Library of Australia, Canberra, MS 9518, Series 1, Volume 13, item 1
Inscribed on the UNESCO Memory of the World Register, 2001

UNESCO
United Nations
Educational, Scientific and
Cultural Organization

Memory of
the World

Challenges to Cook's assertion of British sovereignty over Australia's east coast in 1770 and the subsequent establishment of a penal colony in 1788, led to a significant legal case, brought by five people of Mer (Murray Island) in the Torres Strait: *Mabo and Others v Queensland (No. 2) (1992)*. One of the plaintiffs, Edward Mabo, spent much of his life campaigning for recognition of the traditional ownership of land. This is one of eight maps tendered in evidence. In this landmark case, the High Court of Australia recognised, with qualifications, the traditional ownership of the plaintiffs, and Indigenous land rights more broadly.

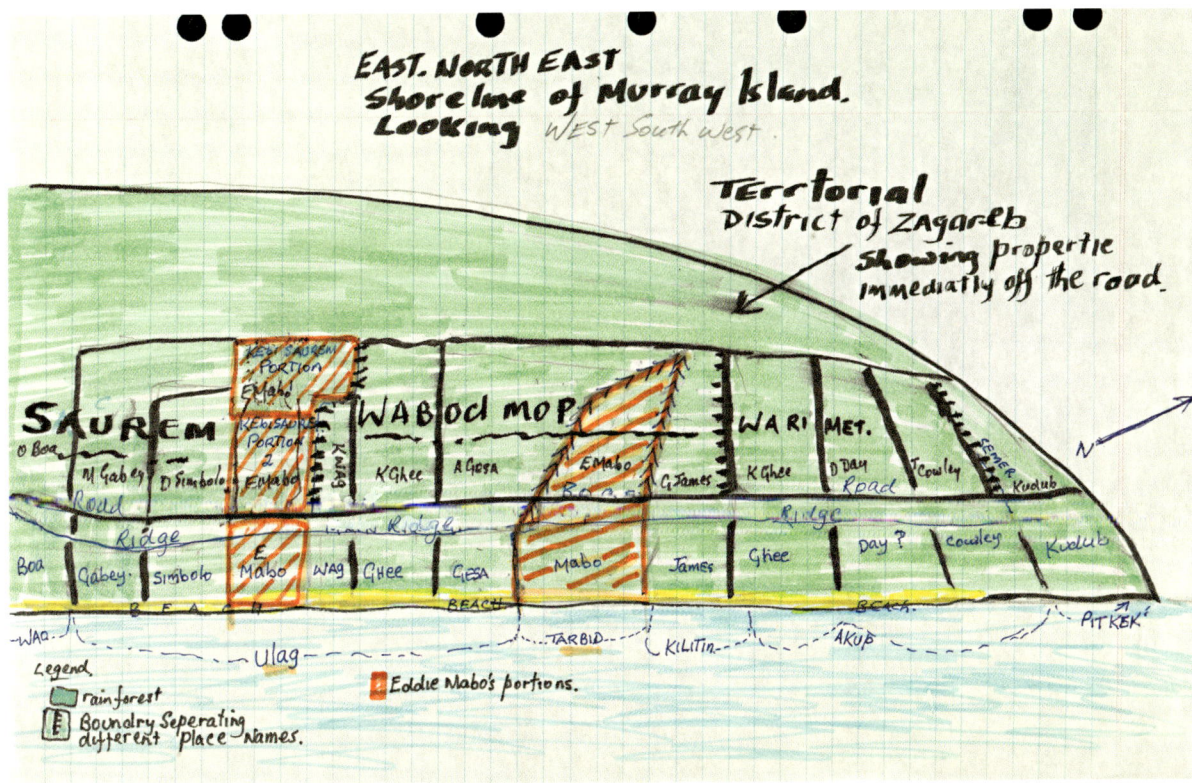

EAST. NORTH EAST Shoreline of Murray Island. Looking WEST South West.

Terrotorial DISTRICT of ZAGAREB Showing properties immediatly off the road.

SAUREM   WABOd MOP.   WARI MET.

Legend.
rainforest
Boundry Seperating different place names.
Eddie Mabo's portions.

177

LEFT

Michel Tuffery (b. 1966)
Cookie from Aotearoa to Mangaia 1777 2011
Courtesy of the artist and Andrew Baker Art Dealer, Brisbane

'After an unfriendly welcome from the people of Mangaia on
29 March 1777, Cookie quickly set sail north landing in Atiu;
he missed the main island of Rarotonga. The hibiscus are a
metaphor for his arrival to what is now known as the Cook
Islands, which I've always personally questioned–how did we
inherit the name 'Cook?"

Michel Tuffery, artist

RIGHT

Karla Dickens (b. 1967)
'The nips are getting bigger/I'd better go get somethin' harder' #5 2015
Courtesy of the artist and Andrew Baker Art Dealer, Brisbane

Michael Cook (b. 1968) Bidjara peoples
Civilised #1 2012
Courtesy of the artist and Andrew Baker Art Dealer, Brisbane

ENDNOTES

'I'm Captain Cooked': Aboriginal perspectives on James Cook, 1770–2020

[1] Stan Grant, 'Between catastrophe and survival: the real journey Captain Cook set us on', ABC News, 25 August 2017: http://www.abc.net.au/news/2017-08-25/stan-grant-captain-cook-indigenous-culture-statues-history/8843172 (accessed 14 February 2018).

[2] 'Additional Instructions for Lt James Cook appointed to Command His Majt's Bark the *Endeavour* (Secret) 30 July 1768', Manuscripts Collection, National Library of Australia, MS 2.

[3] James Cook, *Endeavour* journal, 30 April 1770, Manuscripts Collection, National Library of Australia, MS 1, f. 228v.

[4] James Cook, *Endeavour* journal, 23 August 1770, Manuscripts Collection, National Library of Australia, MS 1, f. 299r.

[5] Deborah Rose, *Hidden Histories,* Aboriginal Studies Press, Canberra, 1991, p. 16; D. Rose, *Dingo Makes Us Human: Life and Land in an Australian Aboriginal Culture,* Cambridge University Press, Cambridge, 2000, p. 189; Minoru Hokari, *Gurindji Journey: A Japanese Historian in the Outback,* UNSW Press, Sydney, 2011, pp. 261–63; Peter Carey, *A Long Way from Home,* Penguin Books, Melbourne, 2017, p. 318.

[6] Terry Crowley, 1973, MS 3102 Finding Aid, Language elicitation from the north coast of NSW [AIATSIS Sound Collection CD 002762-002764], Archive Tape A2764, Track A, Side 1, Field Tape Number 5.

[7] Umbarra Cultural Centre, *View from the Mountain,* (unpublished MS), Wallaga Lake, 1994, p. 8.

[8] Personal recollection by Dr Ray Kelly, Newcastle, 13 November 2017.

[9] Personal recollection, Kelly.

[10] John Maynard, '"Captain Cook came very cheeky you know"—James Cook an Aboriginal appraisal', *East Coast Encounter: Re-imagining 1770,* Lisa Chandler (ed.), One Day Hill Pty Ltd, Collingwood, Vic., 2014, p. 16.

Cook and the Pacific

[1] James Cook, Journal, Sunday 30 January 1774, in J.C. Beaglehole (ed.), *The Journals of Captain James Cook on His Voyages of Discovery.* Vol. II: The Voyage of the *Resolution* and *Adventure* 1772–1775 (Woodbridge: The Boydell Press, 1999 reprint of 1969 Hakluyt Society edition), p. 322.

[2] James Cook, *Endeavour* journal, National Library of Australia, MS 1, f.299r

[3] James Cook, *Endeavour* journal, 30 April 1770, National Library of Australia, MS 1, f.229r.

[4] J.C. Beaglehole (ed.), *The Endeavour Journal of Joseph Banks 1768–1771,* vol. 2 (2nd ed. 1963), Angus & Robertson, Sydney, p. 85.

[5] Official log of the *Endeavour,* British Library, Add MS 8959, f.130v.

[6] 'Secret Additional Instructions for Lt James Cook appointed to Command His Majts Bark the Endeavour', 30 July 1768, in Cook's Voyage 1768–1771: Copies of correspondence, Manuscripts Collection, National Library of Australia, MS 2, unfoliated.

[7] John Hawkesworth, *An Account of the Voyages Undertaken … for Making Discoveries in the Southern Hemisphere*, 3 vols, London, 1773.

[8] Sir James Harris, Letter to Lord Sandwich, St Petersburg 18 January 1780, Manuscripts Collection, National Library of Australia, MS 7218, item 40.

[9] *The Journals of Captain James Cook on His Voyages of Discovery* (ed. J.C. Beaglehole), Hakluyt Society, Cambridge, 1955–74; Bernard Smith, *European Vision and the South Pacific, 1768–1850: A Study in the History of Art and Ideas,* Clarendon Press, Oxford, 1960.

[10] '"Vigils of protest' to greet the Queen: Aboriginals to mourn at Cook gala', *The Australian,* 7 February 1970, p. 3.

FURTHER READING

BOOKS

Barnett, James K., and Nicandri, David L. (eds), *Arctic Ambitions: Captain Cook and the Northwest Passage*. Seattle and London: University of Washington Press, 2015.

Beaglehole, J.C. (ed.), *The Endeavour Journal of Joseph Banks, 1768–1771*. Sydney: The Trustees of the Public Library of New South Wales, in association with Angus and Robertson, 1962.

Beaglehole, J.C. (ed.), *The Journals of Captain James Cook on His Voyages of Discovery*. Woodbridge: The Boydell Press, in association with Hordern House, Sydney, 1999.

Beaglehole, J.C., *The Life of Captain James Cook*. Stanford: Stanford University Press, 1974.

Beddie, M.K. (ed.), *Bibliography of Captain James Cook, RN, FRS, Circumnavigator*, 2nd ed. Sydney: Council of the Library of New South Wales, 1970.

Carter, Harold B., *Sir Joseph Banks 1743–1820*. London: British Museum, 1988.

Chambers, Neil (ed.), *Endeavouring Banks: Exploring Collections from the Endeavour Voyage, 1768–1771*. Sydney: NewSouth Publishing, 2016.

David, Andrew, Joppien, Rüdiger, Smith, Bernard (eds), *The Charts and Coastal Views of Captain Cooks Voyages*, vol. 1: *The Voyage of the Endeavour, 1768–1771*. London: The Hakluyt Society, in association with the Australian Academy of the Humanities, 1988.

Forster, Georg, *A Voyage Round the World*, 2 vols, Thomas, Nicholas, and Berghof, Oliver (eds). Honolulu: University of Hawai'i Press, 2000.

Gascoigne, John, *Captain Cook: Voyager Between Worlds*. London and New York: Hambledon Continuum, 2007.

Hetherington, Michelle, and Morphy, Howard (eds), *Discovering Cook's Collections*. Canberra: National Museum of Australia Press, 2009.

Joppien, Rüdiger, and Smith, Bernard, *The Art of Captain Cook's Voyages: The Voyage of the Resolution and Discovery, 1776–1780*. Melbourne: Oxford University Press, 1987.

Kaeppler, Adrienne L., '*Artificial Curiosities': Being an Expostion of Native Manufactures Collected on the Three Pacific Voyages of Captain James Cook, RN, at the Bernice Pauahi Bishop Museum, January 18, 1978 – August 31, 1978, on the Occasion of the Bicentennial of the European Discovery of the Hawaiian Islands by Captain Cook, January 18, 1778*. Honolulu: Bishop Museum Press, 1978.

Kaeppler, Adrienne L., *Holophusicon: The Leverian Museum: An Eighteenth-Century English Institution of Science, Curiosity, and Art*. Altenstadt: ZKF Publishers, in association with the Museum für Völkerkunde Wien, 2011.

Kaeppler, Adrienne L., and Fleck, Robert (eds), *James Cook and the Exploration of the Pacific*. London: Thames and Hudson, 2009.

Lincoln, Margarette (ed.), *Science and Exploration in the Pacific: European Voyages to the Southern Oceans in the Eighteenth Century*. Woodbridge: The Boydell Press, in association with the National Maritime Museum, Greenwich, 1998.

Matsuda, Matt K., *Pacific Worlds: A History of Seas, Peoples, and Cultures*. Cambridge: Cambridge University Press, 2012.

McAleer, John, and Rigby, Nigel, *Captain Cook and the Pacific: Art, Exploration and Empire*. New Haven: Yale University Press, in association with the National Maritime Museum, Greenwich, 2017.

Newell, Jennifer, *Trading Nature: Tahitians, Europeans, and Ecological Exchange*. Honolulu: University of Hawai'i Press, 2010.

Nugent, Maria, *Captain Cook Was Here*, Melbourne: Cambridge University Press, 2009.

Quilley, Geoffrey, and Bonehill, John (eds), *William Hodges, 1744–1797: The Art of Exploration*. New Haven and London: Yale University Press, 2004.

Richardson, Brian W., *Longitude and Empire: How Captain Cook's Voyages Changed the World*. Vancouver: UBC Press, 2005.

Robson, John, *Captain Cook's World: Maps of the Life and Voyages of James Cook RN*. Milson's Point, NSW: Random House Australia, 2000.

Robson, John, *The Captain Cook Encyclopedia*. London: Chatham Publishing, 2004.

Robson, John, *Captain Cook's War and Peace: The Royal Navy Years, 1755–1768*. Barnsley: Seaforth Publishing, 2009.

Salmond, Anne, *Trial of the Cannibal Dog: Captain Cook in the South Seas*. London: Allen Lane, 2003.

Salmond, Anne, *Aphrodite's Island: The European Discovery of Tahiti*. Auckland: Viking, 2009.

Thomas, Nicholas, *Discoveries: The Voyages of Captain Cook*. London: Penguin, 2004.

Williams, Glyndwr (ed.), *Captain Cook: Explorations and Reassessments*. Rochester: The Boydell Press, 2004.

Williams, Glyn[dwr] (ed.), *The Death of Captain Cook: A Hero Made and Unmade*. London: Profile Books, 2008.

WEBSITES

The Captain Cook Society: captaincooksociety.com

South Seas Voyaging and Cross-Cultural Encounters in the Pacific (1760–1800): southseas.nla.gov.au

INDEX

Page numbers in italics indicate an illustration; those in bold, an illustration with an accompanying description. Locations are indexed under their current English names when these appear in the text. Exhibition items are listed under their creator where applicable. Titles have been shortened; to save further space, ellipses indicating words missing from the beginnings and ends of titles have been omitted.

Aboriginal and Torres Strait Islander peoples, 1–3, 8, 13, 20, 88, 89, **92**, **93**, **96**, 161, 175, 176
Additional Instructions for Lt James Cook, 2, 9
Adventure (ship), 11, 38, 141
Adventure Bay, Tas., **104–5**, 106
Ansell, Ronnie, *Aboriginals Discovered Cook*, *184*
Antarctic Circle, 83, *84*
Antill's Corroboree, **172**
Apotheosis of Captain Cook, 154, *155*
Armidale, NSW, 3
Arnold, John, 11; *Maritime Chronometers*, **44**
Asia, 11, 114
Australia (New Holland), 1–3, 5, 7–9, 13, 14, 20, 86–113, 158, 177
Australian National Travel Association, *Australia's 150th Anniversary*, **170**

Banks, Joseph, 8, 9, 11, 12, 45, **109**, 113, **140**, **164**; *Vocabulary ... Guugu Yimithirr People*, 15
Barralet, John James, 58
Barrington, Daines, 149, 151; *Letter to Lord Sandwich*, **149**
Batavia, 88, 93, 103
Bay of Islands, New Zealand, 68
Beaglehole, J.C., 13, 174
Bookshelf of Works, **174**
Boomali Aboriginal Artists Co-operative, *Captain Cook*, **175**
Boomerangs, **94–5**
Botany Bay, NSW, *3*, 8, 9, **90**, **91**, 92, *110*, **171**
Brindle, Bill, *Re-enactment of the Landing*, **171**
Broadside Announcing the Death of ... Cook, **133**
Bruny Island, Tas., 104
Burney, James, *Map of Van Demen's Land*, 9
Byrne, William, *New Caledonia*, **76–7**

Caldwall, James, '*Man of Van Diemen's Land*', 106, *107*
Cameron, Sandy, 2
Cannon from HMB Endeavour, **38**
canoes, 10, 11, **29**, *32*, **33**, **34–5**, *92*, *93*
Captain Cook's Scale of Sines, **42**
Carter, George, *Death of Captain Cook*, **122–3**
Carved Ivory Female Figure, 75

Catalogue of ... Webber, 152, 153
Catherine the Great, 12, 132, 135
Certificate Recommending ... James Cook, 45, *46*
Chambers, Thomas, *Chief of New Zealand*, **63**
charts (maps): Australia, *9*, **87**, **90**, **98**, **177**; New Zealand, *66*, *67*, *68*; North America, *6*, **22**; North Pacific, 118, *119*; South Pacific, 29, *30–1*, **52**; southern hemisphere, *84*, *85*; world, 155, *156–7*, **162–3**
Chest of New Zealand, 73
'*Chief Mourner's*' *Costume*, 58, *59*
Clerke, Charles, 125, 126, 146; *Log*, **125**
Cleveley, John, 65; *Discovery and Resolution*, **64–5**
clubs, 72, **94–5**
Cohan, George, '*If Captain Cook should come to life*', **168**
Companion to the Museum, **148**
Contemporary Plan of the Resolution, **40–1**
Cook, Elizabeth, 12, 132, 135, 136, 138; *Letter to Lord Sandwich*, 135, *136*; *Waistcoat of Tahiti Cloth*, 136, *137*
Cook, James, 1–3, 5–13, 18, 25, 45, 146; Australia, 86, 87, 99; *Coat of Arms*, **138**; death, 10, 12, 114, 118, **122–3**, **125**, 132, **133–6**; drawings, *6*, **22**, *52*, *66*, *67*, *84*, *85*, **87**; images of, *3*, *4*, *19*, **122–3**, *139*, 154, *155*, *159*, *175*, *178*; North America, 21, 22; North Pacific, 114, 118, 123; South Pacific, 47, 52, 63, 74, 76, 83, 85; works after, **101**; writings, 8, *17*, **21**, 38, *39*, 44, 45, **49**, **100**, *117*, **124**
Cook, Michael, 20; *Civilised #1*, **179**; *Undiscovered #4*, **20**
Cook's Box of Instruments, 5
Cook's Holograph Journal, 44, 45
Copperplate Engraving of Grevillea, **113**
Coral Concretion from ... Cannon, 38
Cronulla, NSW, 172

Darly, Matthew, *Macaroni* prints, **164**
De Loutherbourg, Philippe Jacques, 12, 132, 154, *155*; *Chief Mourner Otahaite*, 7; *Drums Otaheite* (attrib.), 144, *145*; *Toha, Chief of Otahaite*, **144**
Dickens, Karla, '*The nips are getting bigger*', *13*, *178*
Discovery (ship), 11, 54, **64–5**, **104**, 114
Douglas, James, 4th Earl of Morton, *Hints Offered to ... Captain Cooke*, **27**
Douglas, John, 12

Easter Island (Rapa Nui), 10, 62, **78–9**
Elliott, John, 146; '*Officers and Civilians on ... Resolution*', **146**; *Resolution*, **147**
Ellis, William Wade, 11, 114; *Adventure Bay*, **104–5**; *Kamchatka*, **126**; *Oitapeeah Bay*, **60–1**; *Ship Cove*, **116**; *Winter View of Kamtschatska*, **127**

Endeavour (ship), 9, 11, **24–5**, **36–7**, 38, 98; *Cannon*, **38**; *Coral Concretion*, 38; *Journal*, 15, **100**, **101**; *Muster Book*, **103**; *Official Log*, **102**
Endeavour Reef, Qld, 37, 38
Endeavour River (Waalumbaal Birri), Qld, 9, 14, **98**, *99*, 101, 110, *111*
Faden, William, *Chart ... Isles of the South Sea*, 29, *30–1*
fauna, **91**, *99*, **106**, *108*, 109, **120**
First Nations peoples, 5–6, 8, 13, 14, 18. *See also* Aboriginal and Torres Strait Islander peoples; Maori; *specific place names*
flora, **54**, **110**, *111*, **112–13**
Fly Ansett Airlines of Australia, **173**
Forster, Georg, 76, 150, **151**
Forster, Johann Reinhold, 12, 76, 146, 150, **151**; *Account of a Voyage*, **150**
French Paper ... Plates to the Voyage, 153
funerary rituals, 58, *59*

George III, 132; *Minute ... to Lord Sandwich*, **134**
Grant, Stan, 1
Great Barrier Reef, Qld, 9, 38
Green, Charles, 6, 47, 49, 103
Grevillea pteridifolia, 110, *111*, **112–13**
Griffith, Moses, 109; *Rainbow Lorikeet*, *108*, 109
Grignion, Charles, *Canoe ... Sandwich Islands*, 33

Halley, Edmond, 47
Harbour Grace, Newfoundland, **22**
Harris, James, 1st Earl of Malmesbury, *Letter to Lord Sandwich*, **135**
Harvey, William, *Death of James Cook*, **125**
Hawaii (Sandwich Islands), 10, 14, **33**, 114, **118**, *119*, 123, 124, *145*
Hawkesworth, John, 12, 100
Hikiau Heiau, Hawaii, 118
Hodges, William, 49, 50, 78, 146; *Chart ... Southern Hemisphere*, *84*, *85*; *Man of Easter Island*, **79**; *Man of New Caledonia*, **77**; *Man of Tanna*, 80, *81*; *Maori Chieftain*, **69**; *Maori Man*, **85**; *Otoo, King of Otaheite*, 50, *51*; *Tynai-mai*, **50**; *View from Point Venus*, iv, *48*, 49; *Woman and Child of Tanna*, vi, *81*; *Woman of Easter Island*, 78, *79*; *Woman of New Caledonia*, *77*; *Woman of New Zealand*, **69**; works after, *29*, *32*, *76–7*, *78–9*, *80–1*, *82–3*
Horner, Arthur, '*This is the place for a cottage*', **166**
Hyde, Miriam, *Captain Cook Sketchbook*, **169**

instruments used by Cook, 5, 7, **23**, **42**, **44**

journals, 5, 8, 9, 12, 13, 14, *15–17*, 44, 45, **70–1**, 89, **100**, **101**, **117**

Ka'awaloa, Hawaii, 118
Kamchatka, Russia, **126–31**

Kealakekua Bay, Hawaii, 10, 114, **118**, *119*, 123, 125
Kendall, Larcum, 11, 44
King, James, 12, 131
Kurnell, NSW, **171**, 172

Lansac, Regis, *Anti-bicentenary Demonstration*, **176**
Late Victorian Copy … Cook's 1789 Coat of Arms, **138**
letters, 26, 27, 38, *39*, **134**, **135**, *136*, **148**, 149
Lever, Ashton, **148**
List Showing the Engravers, **154**
logs, 102, 124, 125
Luny, Thomas, *Endeavour*, 24–5

Mabo, Edward Koiki, *Map … Murray Island*, **177**
Mahiole (Helmet), **121**
Mai (Omai), 6–7, 12, **141**, *142*
Maori, 7, 62, **63**, 69, **70–1**, 85
maps see charts (maps)
Marquesas Islands, 10, 62
Maskelyne, Nevil, 11, 45; *Nautical Almanac and Astronomical Ephemeris*, 11, **43**
Maynard, John, *Graffiti*, viii
Mere Pounamu (Flat, Broad Club), 72
Middiman, Samuel, *Venus Fort*, 48
Miller, John Frederick, 97, 113; *Five Spears and a Shield*, **97**; *Grevillea pteridifolia*, **112–13**; works after, 56, 73
Miniature Celestial Globe, 7
Molnar, George, 'All this pommy showing-off', **165**
Montagu, John, 4th Earl of Sandwich, 148, 149, 150; *Letter to Sir Joseph Banks*, **148**
Mount Dromedary (Gulaga), NSW, 8
Myrtaceae Callistemon citrinus, *110*

navigation, 11–12, 21, 28, 29, **42**, **43**, 88
New Caledonia, 10, 62, **76–7**
New Guinea, **97**
New South Wales, 9, **87**, **88**, 102
New Zealand (Aotearoa), 5, 7, 9, 10, 14, 62, **63**, **66–73**, 85, 97
Newfoundland, Canada, 18, **22**
Nootka Sound, 11, **115**, **116**, *117*
North America, 21, **22**, 114
North Pacific, 10, 14, 114–31
Northfield, James, *Discover Australia*, **170**
Northwest Passage, 5, 10, 114
Nova Scotia, Canada, 18, 22

Official Log of the Endeavour, **102**
Omai, or a Trip Round the World, 7, *132*, **143**
Orton, Richard, 100; *Endeavour Journal*, **101**

Pacific, 5–13, 18, 26, 28–33, **64–5**, 158
Pahoa (Dagger), **122–3**
Parkinson, Sydney, 63, 91, 103, 112; *Bread Fruit* (attrib.), **54**; *Green Turtle*, **99**; *Grevillea pteridifolia*, **112**; *Two Australian Aboriginal People*, **92**; *Vocabulary …*

People of New Holland, *16*; works after, *48*, *58*, *63*, **112–13**
Pennant, Thomas, 12, 109; *Animals Observed or Collected*, **109**
Phillip, Arthur, 170
Pickersgill, Richard, 8, 68, 89, 146; *Chart … New Zealand*, **68**; *Journal*, **89**; *Plan of Sting-ray Bay*, **90**; *Plan … River on the East Coast of New Holland*, **98**
Pigeon House Mountain (Didthul), NSW, 8, **88**, 89
Pingo, Lewis, *Commemorative Medal*, **140**
Plane Table Frame, 42
Playbill for 'Omai', **143**
Poetua (Poedua), 54, 55
Point Hicks, Vic., 8, 9
Point Venus, Tahiti, *iv*, 47, 48, 49
Poole, Thomas R., *Captain James Cook*, **139**
Port Resolution, Vanuatu, 80
Possession Island, Qld, 1, 9
Pouilly, T., *Brass Graphometer*, **23**
Pouncy, Benjamin Thomas, *Ice Islands*, **82–3**
Poverty Bay, New Zealand, 7, 63
Praval, Charles, 88, 103; *Australian Aboriginal Person*, **96**; *New South Wales*, **88**
Presents for Omai, 142
Prince William Sound, 11, **34–5**, 118
Proteaceae Grevillea pteridifolia, 110, *111*, **112–13**
Pryor, Geoff, 'Let's hope the natives are friendly', **167**

Ra'iatea, 50, 54, 55
Ralph, R., 73
Reconciliation Rocks, Qld, 99
Resolution (ship), 11, 38, **40–1**, **64–5**, *84*, 85, **104**, 114, **116**, 146, **147**; 'Officers and Civilians', **146**
Resolution and Adventure Medal, 104, *105*
Reynolds, Joshua, *Omai of the Friendly Isles*, **141**
Rigaud, Jean François, *Johann Reinhold Forster and … Georg Forster*, **151**
Riou, Edward, *Kara'ka'hooah [Kealakekua] Bay*, 118, *119*
Roberts, Henry: *Chart of the Southern Hemisphere*, 84, 85; *General Chart … Discoveries Made by … Cook*, 155, 156–7
Rose, Ray, 1
Ruff, Carol, *Aboriginals Discovered Cook*, 184

Salmon, Michael, *G'day Captain Cook*, **161**
Samwell, David, 14, 70, 130; *Journal*, **70–1**
Sharp, William, *Night Dance*, **74–5**
Sherwin, John Keyes, *Landing at Tanna*, 80–1
ship plans, **36–7**, **40–1**
Smith, Isaac, *Chart … New Zealand*, 66, 67
Society Islands (Totaiete mā), 47–61, *136*
Solander, Daniel, 9, 103, **109**, 110, 148, **164**

South Pacific, 14, *30–1*, 62–85, **147**
Spöring, Herman Diedrich, 91, 103; *Urolophus testaceus*, **91**
Staffordshire Figurine … James Cook, **159**
Stephens, Philip, *Letter to James Cook*, **26**

Ta (Tahitian Tattooing Implement), **57**
Tahiti (Otahaite, Otaheite), *iv*, 6, **29**, 32, 33, 47–52, **57**, **58**, **60–1**, *136*, **144**, *145*
Tahitian Tattooing Mallet, **57**
Tanna, Vanuatu, *vi*, **80–1**
Tasmania (Van Diemen's Land), 9, 86, **104–7**
tattooing, **57**, **63**, **69**
Täumi (Breast Ornament), **53**, **144**
Three Ivory Turtle Ornaments, **120**
Tonga (Friendly Islands), 10, 32, 33, 62, **74–5**, **141**
Tools from the Society Islands, 56
transit of Venus, 6, 47, 49
Trompf, Percy, *Landing … at Botany Bay*, 3
Tu (Otoo), 50, *51*
Tucker, Alan, *Too Many Captain Cooks*, **161**
Tuffery, Michel: *Cookie from Aotearoa to Mangaia 1777*, **178**; *Cookie in Te Wai Pounamu*, *4*
Tupaia, 6, 7, 28, 29, *30–1*, 103; *Australian Aboriginal People*, **93**
Turanganui River, New Zealand, 62
Tynai-mai, 50

Vanuatu (New Hebrides), 10, 62, **80–1**
View in the Island of Otaheite, **58**
Voyages to the Southern Hemisphere, **160**

Walker, Kath (Oodgeroo Noonuccal), 13
Wallis, Samuel, 6, 47
Watts, William, *Boats of the Friendly Isles*, 32, 33
weaponry, **38**, 72, **94–5**, **97**, **122–3**
Webber, John, 11, 12, 19, 74, 114; *Canoe of Otaheite*, 32, 33; *Captain James Cook*, **19**; *Catalogue*, 152, 153; *Indians of Nootka Sound*, **115**; *Kamchatka Winter Habitation*, **130**; *Kealakekua Bay*, **118**; *Man of Kamschatka*, *129*; *Opossum of Van Diemen's Land*, **106**; *People of Prince William Sound*, **34–5**; *Poedua*, 54, *55*; *Travelling in Kamtschatka*, **131**; *Woman of Kamschatka*, 128, 129; works after, **33**, **74–5**, 106, *107*, **144**, *145*, 152, 153, 154, *155*
Wedgwood, *Joseph Banks*, **140**
Wedgwood and Bentley, *Captain Cook*, **139**
Weston, Miss, *Map of the World*, **162–3**
Whitby, United Kingdom, 11, **24–5**
Wooden Wahaika (Short Club), 72
wordlists, 14, *15*, *16*, *17*, 117
Woollett, William: *Fleet of Otaheite*, **29**; *Monuments of Easter Island*, 78–9

ACKNOWLEDGEMENTS

The Library acknowledges the generous assistance of the following people, communities and institutions:

International lenders: The National Archives (UK), The British Library, London; Royal Society, London; National Maritime Museum, Greenwich, London; Natural History Museum, London; Captain Cook Memorial Museum, Whitby; Museum of New Zealand Te Papa Tongarewa, Wellington; Alexander Turnbull Library, Wellington; Bernice Pauahi Bishop Museum, Honolulu.

Domestic lenders: National Gallery of Australia, Canberra; National Portrait Gallery, Canberra; National Museum of Australia, Canberra; Parliament House Art Collection, Department of Parliamentary Services, Canberra; State Library of New South Wales, Sydney; Australian Museum, Sydney; Australian National Maritime Museum Sydney; The Royal Botanic Gardens and Domain Trust, National Herbarium of New South Wales, Sydney; Martyn Cook Antiques, Sydney; State Library Victoria, Melbourne; Kerry Stokes Collection, Perth; Michel Tuffery courtesy Andrew Baker Art Dealer, Brisbane; and one private lender.

First Nations communities: The Ngunawal, Ngunnawal and Ngambri Communities of the Canberra region; Aboriginal and Torres Strait Islander colleagues at the National Library of Australia; Shane Carriage and Victor Channell, Ulladulla Local Aboriginal Land Council; Alberta Hornsby and Loretta Sullivan, Cooktown; Natea Montillier Tetuanui, Tahiti, Cultural office of French Polynesia; Margarita James and Kevin Kowalchuk, Mowachaht/ Muchalaht First Nation; Nicholas Chin and Wendy Hynes, Rangitane, New Zealand; Stella Pahulu Naimet, Sioana Faupula, Manutu'ufanga Naufahu and Toa Fulivai Takiari, Tongan community of Canberra; and numerous others.

Carol Ruff (project coordinator and designer) and
Ronnie Ansell (designer)
Muneena from Borroloola (detail from mural)
Adelaide Festival Centre 1982
Courtesy of the artist and Adelaide Festival Centre